GHOST INVESTIGATOR

Volume 13

Written by
Linda Zimmermann

Linda Zimmermann's Facebook Fan Page

http://www.facebook.com/pages/Linda-Zimmermann/116636310250

The author is always looking for new ghost stories. If you would like to share a haunting experience or find out more about her work, go to:

www.ghostinvestigator.com

Or write to:

Linda Zimmermann
P.O. Box 192
Blooming Grove, NY 10914

Or send email to:

lindazim@optonline.net

What else is Linda Zimmermann writing? Go to: www.gotozim.com

Ghost Investigator: Volume 13

Copyright © 2015 Linda Zimmermann

All rights reserved. This book may not be reproduced in whole or in part without permission.

ISBN: 978-1-937174-26-2

CONTENTS

Bodine's Tavern   1

Butchered and Burned?   15

St. John's-in-the-Wilderness   21

Buyer Beware   30

Gone, But Never Forgotten   34

Montgomery Firehouse   46

House Call   56

Desmond House Revisited   69

North Church Street   79

Museum Village   81

Websites:

Linda Zimmermann:
www.gotozim.com

Barbara Roth Bleitzhofer:
www.barbrothreadings.com

Michael Worden:
www.michaeljworden.com

Bodine's Tavern
Montgomery, NY

You just can't buy charm, character, or good taste, but thanks to the picturesque architecture and the talents of owner Yvonne Comeau, this former tavern has all three in abundance. It also has something else you can't buy—an abundance of ghosts.

Around 1806, Adam and Anna Bodine built this place on the new Middletown-Minisink Turnpike (which eventually became Route 211) by a popular crossing point in the Wallkill River. Long before there was a bridge, this fording spot allowed people traveling on foot, horseback, or in a carriage or wagon, to traverse this natural obstacle if the water levels were not too high. And before you got your feet wet, you might as well wet your whistle at Bodine's Tavern, have your horses looked after at the blacksmith shop, or even spend the night in the adjacent inn.

It became a very popular destination—even if you weren't traveling—and one can only imagine the people gathering here for a pint of ale, a hot meal, and all the latest news and gossip. The Bodines sold the property in

1835, and eventually the tavern and inn became private homes. The blacksmith shop fell into ruins, and the tavern was in threat of a similar fate, as the man who bought the place in the 1950s told Yvonne that it was "uninsurable and uninhabitable." It stood vacant for a considerable amount of time until extensive renovations were completed. However, the original woodwork, floors, and beams remained intact, as did the footprint of the house, with no added rooms.

When Yvonne, a collector of primitive and antique furniture for many years, saw the house, she knew it was the place for her. After she had decided to buy it, she showed the place to her brother, Chris, who it is very sensitive to spirits.

"Good luck, Yvonne," he told her as they stood inside the old tavern. "I hope you like ghosts"

"Oh, Chris, don't say that!" Yvonne replied, clearly not happy with the prospect of sharing her home with unseen inhabitants.

"No, really, there are ghosts here."

"Come on, I don't need you telling me that! I haven't even closed yet."

"Don't worry, they can't wait for you to get here."

"Really? Why?"

"They know you will fix up the place."

Chris was right, as for all the good intentions of the former owners, they didn't all quite keep the interior decoration in harmony with the early 1800s style of the structure. Yvonne explained that bright, mint green paint was everywhere. In fact, one friend complained that it was so bright it hurt his eyes. There was also fancy toile fabric wallpaper depicting Victorian ladies and gentlemen, which actually doesn't sound appropriate for any décor!

"I painted everything with Benjamin Moore historic colors," Yvonne explained, "and hand-stenciled these patterns according to the period."

Her collection of antique furniture, household items, and decorative objects completed the restoration back to how this place might have looked when the Bodines were in residence. And speaking of the Bodines, visitors to the house have told Yvonne that they can feel that Mrs. Bodine is still in her kitchen.

Many people have also commented on the psychic energy in the main hallway, which used to be the entrance to the tavern. People have felt a cool breeze pass them as if someone just walked by. And Yvonne's dog, Princess, often looks down that hall and cocks her head as if she is watching someone.

The main hallway and front door.

One day, Yvonne's four-year-old granddaughter was visiting and was playing upstairs for a while. When she came back downstairs she asked, "Who it is the little girl that wants to play with me?" But there were no other children in the house that day.

On another occasion, Yvonne and her sister were returning from shopping and went into the kitchen to start unpacking what they had bought. From the adjacent dining room, Yvonne clearly heard a man's voice in a singsong manner say, "La la la la."

"Did you hear that?" Yvonne asked her sister.

"You mean the 'La la la la'?" she replied, obviously having heard the same ghost musically announcing his presence.

One of my favorite ghost stories about the old tavern doesn't actually involve a ghost. One afternoon, Yvonne was standing outside when the UPS delivery truck pulled up. The driver seemed to be in a particular hurry as he raced to the front door, put down the package, spun around and started to head back to the truck when he sighted Yvonne standing nearby.

"Jesus Christ! What are you doing here?" the terrified man asked, having practically jumped out of his skin.

"I live here," Yvonne replied rather amused, but puzzled.

"I thought you were a ghost!" the shaken man said, and then continued. "This place is so haunted!"

With that, the man jumped back into his truck and sped away. Apparently sometime in the past, he either saw a ghost at the old tavern, or experienced something that so unnerved him he is still reluctant to make deliveries there.

While Yvonne's brother is not unnerved by the many spirits at Bodine's Tavern, they clearly don't like him for some reason, perhaps because he admittedly "snoops around" into their business. He has described on several occasions receiving a "psychic slap" when he was in the house. One of the more dramatic events occurred after he and his wife had spent some time visiting Yvonne.

Saying goodbye to Chris and his wife in the driveway as they pulled away, Yvonne then went back into the house, which in her words, suddenly "reeked of decay." A friend who was with her at the time also smelled the horrible stench, and finding no logical source for the terrible odor, had to conclude that the spirits had been very annoyed by her brother's presence and were indicating that they would prefer it if he didn't return.

In the middle of the night when Yvonne was in bed, she heard someone tapping on the original tavern door. She simply yelled out, "Go away! The tavern has been closed for 200 years!" and the taping stopped! Was some wandering spirit looking for spirits of another kind to quench his thirst on his long after-death journey?

Among the many other things that occur here, there are sharp changes in temperature. For example, Yvonne can enter the house and find it feeling very cold, but as soon as she announces that she is home, it warms suddenly as if the spirits are welcoming her! Several children have been seen, sometimes in the form of very dark figures. Also, Yvonne and other family members watched in great surprise as a little Super Ball came bouncing down the stairs one day, even though no one had any idea where the ball came from.

Obviously, after hearing all these stories, I knew this was a place I had to investigate. We arranged, on rather short notice, to meet at the house on the Sunday after Christmas in 2014, and I was delighted when Barbara Bleitzhofer said she could come, as well. However, before I describe our visit, I have to relate a very strange experience I had the night before.

Saturday night, I had a very vivid dream about standing in a room of Bodine's tavern, but not in current times. There was a small woman in old-fashioned clothing and a long apron, pointing to a large stain on the wide plank floor. She appeared to be quite agitated and upset by this stain, and she told me, "This is where someone died."

I woke up with a start and wondered what the heck was *that* all about? But I have been doing this too long to dismiss such things. In the morning, I told my husband, Bob, all about my dream, and I asked him to remind me to look for stains, if there were any wide plank floors still remaining in the house. And wouldn't you know, this would all lead to an astonishing revelation. But more on that later.

It was a cold morning when Bob and I arrived, and it was wonderful to enter the side door of the house into the original tap room of the tavern with its cozy fire in the wood stove in the corner. Unlike the majority of haunted places I investigate, this place was literally and figuratively warm and inviting, and it just gave me the impression that this had been a very happy and lively place. Yvonne has really worked her magic here, and it feels like you are truly stepping back 200 years when you enter the house. The period furnishings and décor are done just right, and it is no wonder that the spirits of Bodine's Tavern are thrilled to have Yvonne taking care of their beloved home!

A warm fire greeted us.

Barbara arrived shortly after and exclaimed, "This is gorgeous! And very loud!"

She explained that on the drive there, she was receiving a lot of messages and many spirits were talking at once. Some of the messages were personal for Yvonne from family members. For example, she asked if her father had been in uniform, because that's the way he was appearing to Barb and he seemed to be very proud of his service. Yvonne explained that not only had her father been proud to serve in the army, but had also been a police officer for many years.

Other messages had been less specific, such as the person who had a serious breathing disorder, some connection with Japan, and the distinct command that, "Carol has to go!" Yvonne doesn't know anyone named Carol, or of any connection with Japan, so perhaps these were situations involving previous owners, or things that have not yet occurred.

We all admired the original woodwork and fireplaces, and I took particular interest in the wide plank floors and a stain that appeared in the tavern room, but I didn't want to mention my dream quite yet. I wanted to see what Barbara had to say first—which was plenty, as the spirits here have "a lot of energy, are very loud, and jubilant."

"Do you hear music?" Barbara asked.

Yvonne related the story of hearing the melodious man in the dining room, and also mentioned that she usually keeps her XM Radio on all day long.

"They like the music," Barb said after listening for a moment. "It reminds them of the good times they used to have in the tavern."

In the kitchen, where many people have commented on the presence of Mrs. Bodine, Barbara felt the strong female presence of a woman who was rather small in stature, and was very sweet-natured. When we went into the dining room, Barb immediately looked at an upholstered chair in the corner and declared, "*He* sits in that chair. *He* likes to look out there." Could this have been Adam Bodine, looking out the window for customers? She also mentioned that there was a woman who enjoys sitting in the rocking chair. Yvonne had already been told that before, but rather than being Mrs. Bodine, Barb identified the woman as Betsy.

At this point, Bob started getting some high EMF readings by the pantry between the kitchen and dining room. He couldn't find any appliances or electrical lines to explain the readings, and they eventually faded. Perhaps we momentarily stirred up someone?

"They used to hold a lot of talks in here," Barbara explained. "A lot of political big shots would come here to drink and discuss the important matters of the day. I'm even hearing that they would hold judgment here. I wouldn't be surprised if you found out a lot of the local politicians used to meet here."

Then once again, Barbara declared, "Carol must go!" I feel sorry for anyone named Carol who ever tries to visit Yvonne!

Barbara and Yvonne discuss the spirits in the kitchen.

Barb had to pause again as so much information was streaming to her. She spoke about army encampments in the area, as well as Indian camps from long ago, being on this property, all adding to the intense energy of the place. She said there were many children's spirits there, and a man who had sustained a war injury and, as a result, dragged his foot.

"But there's nothing to worry about here," Barb told Yvonne. "It's all very uplifting energy, and a lot of laughter. And they *love* you, because you are doing a bang-up job with the place!"

The dining room where Barbara saw the man sitting in the chair to the left of the fireplace. The rocking chair is in the opposite corner.

The bathroom is a modern addition, but Barbara believes that this room was once where the cook used to sleep when the place was a tavern. Fortunately, there has not been any major activity here. Some places need to remain private!

On our way down to the cellar, Barbara encountered a younger man named Billy, whom she felt was a pleasant man with a very good sense of humor. He was apparently quite amused that we were there and was happy to get our attention.

There was a large fireplace in the cellar, where a lot of the cooking for the tavern used to take place. Barb felt a stream of energy going from that fireplace to a nearby door that led to the property behind the house.

"A lot of people went in and out here," Barb said, as if she was actually watching them hurrying with trays of food. "They would bring food out there and people would eat on blankets."

Other people had told Yvonne this, that especially in the warmer months, food would be brought out from the cellar kitchen to people resting in the shade of the trees by the river. It must have been quite pleasant to escape the dust and heat of the old Minnisink-Middletown Turnpike and then rest your weary bones, and have a cool pint of ale, or two, or three…

So far, our investigation had not uncovered anything negative. But that was about to change, and in quite a dramatic fashion. As we stepped into the part of the basement facing the road, the atmosphere took a decidedly unpleasant turn, which we all experienced, but Barbara verbalized it best, "Whoa! Not good!"

Someone had clearly died here and remained here, because they were angry with themselves that they had caused their own death. Yvonne confirmed that there had been a car crash about 1970, killing the driver.

"Had he been drunk?" I suggested.

"That's what I was thinking," Barb agreed. "He won't bother anyone in the house, but he stays down here because he is angry at his own stupidity."

Such experiences are literally sobering, when one considers that our mistakes in life follow us after death—as well as continue to impact the living for many years to come. At least in this case, the accident victim is not taking out his anger on the residents of the house, which is more than I can say for a lot of accident and suicide victim ghosts.

There was a small storage area in the cellar where Barb kept hearing men talking about hiding ammunition, and perhaps even hiding themselves.

"Is there a trapdoor leading down here somewhere?" Barb asked Yvonne. "I hear them saying they have to lower themselves through the trapdoor."

"Yes!" Yvonne replied. "There's a trapdoor in the dining room that comes right down here."

At this point, I decided to finally pose the question I had wanted to ask from the moment I arrived, but I didn't want to ask it in a leading fashion, if at all possible.

"Are there any unusual stains on the wood floors?" I asked Yvonne, and was not quite prepared for her response.

"Yes, there's a large blood stain on the tavern room floor. Someone died there."

Bob and I exchanged glances, and Barb looked to me for further explanation. I told them about my vivid dream, with the woman pointing to the stain on the wide plank floor and telling me that someone died there. Barbara asked if the woman in my dream was wearing old-fashioned clothing and an apron, to which I replied in the affirmative. We went back upstairs to the tavern room and the spot on the floor, and Barb knelt down so that she could place her hands on the stain. It was kind of extra creepy because as I watched, I was standing in the same place as I had stood in my dream. And I had never been in this place before that day!

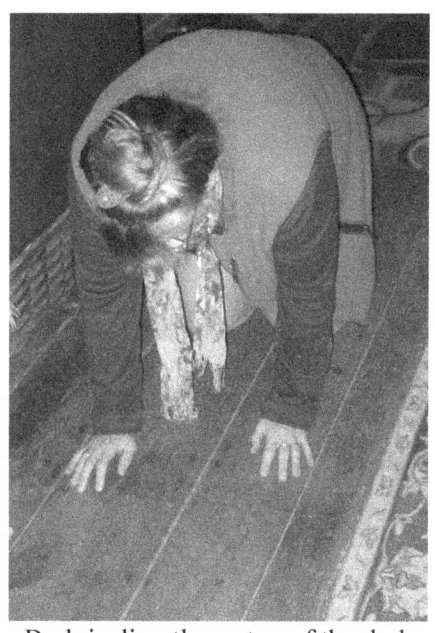

Barb is directly on top of the dark stain to feel its vibes.

"I don't get the sense that it was violent," Barb said thoughtfully. "I think he just had too much drink, fell, and hit his head. The woman was very broken up about it, but he is telling me he was 'just a common man.' He didn't seem to value his own life too much."

I didn't have much time to ponder all the implications of this during the middle of the investigation, but later, the wonder of it all became even more evident. Somehow, the spirits knew we were coming the next day, and had the ability to contact me in my home, in my own bed, while I was sleeping, to give me this important information which would act as conclusive confirmation of their presence! How freakin' cool is *that*!? I know that for Barbara, this kind of stuff happens to her every day, but for me, it is still a very big deal. And it's experiences such as these that keep me going as a ghost investigator.

We next headed upstairs where Barb felt that a small room was where the spirits of the children gather. Yvonne felt this as well, and it is also up here where her granddaughter sees the little girl who wants to play. When Barb first arrived, she had mentioned someone with breathing problems. She now connected that ailment with a nine-year-old girl who died in the house, and was most likely the one who appeared to Yvonne's granddaughter. But she was just one of several children whose spirits had not yet left the building.

When Barb tried to go into Yvonne's bedroom, she felt as though she was being pushed backward and was clearly not welcome.

"My brother feels the same thing here," Yvonne said. "Who is it, and how come I don't feel that?"

Barbara stated that it was the "man of the house" and he didn't like anyone intruding into his private domain. But he doesn't bother Yvonne, because she is taking care of the place that he loves.

While we were upstairs, Barbara once again heard the name Burt or Bart (she had heard the name on the drive over), as well as Jackson and Thomas. I report these names here, in case research in the future uncovers someone with those names connected with this place.

We went outside and walked around the grounds for a while, and Barbara "heard" that there were quite a few spirits that "mosey around the property." These people may or may not have been connected with the old tavern, or had some other, possibly even older, connections with the property.

The carriage house had been remodeled years ago into an unheated, three-season house, and Yvonne's son was currently doing a wonderful job of renovating it into a year-round home. We went inside, and this place definitely did not have the same cozy and inviting feeling of the main house.

"This feels totally different in here," Barb said with an unpleasant expression, as if she was smelling something bad. "There's a sour scent in here. The energy is very stiff and stern. Someone died in here and he wasn't very nice."

Yvonne described an old Russian couple who used to live here, and said that they never bathed. They were also not the nicest people, and she believed that the man did indeed die in this carriage house. This may seem bizarre, but this is actually not the first case I've worked on where body odor was a calling card for an unsanitary ghost! Fortunately, Barbara believes that once the renovations are completed and Yvonne's son moves in, these spirits will move on.

Me, Yvonne, and Barbara: The Ghost Ladies!

We went back into the main house and tried to sum up all of the activity we had experienced that day, as well as everything that had occurred since Yvonne bought the place in 2008. I asked about footsteps and figures she might have encountered, but she said that for the most part, she seems to be oblivious to most of the activity, although her children see and hear things all the time. Perhaps it is just a case of Yvonne being accepted as a member of this extended paranormal family, and they spare her the apparitions and most of the sound effects that usually constitute a haunting.

While I still adhere to the belief that all spirits should move on to better things, there is a harmony between the living and the dead at the old Bodine's Tavern that is somewhat comforting. Potential home buyers are often drawn to a property because of some subtle connection with the people and events from the past, but all too often that connection involves a lot of negative energy. Again, this place is an exception. Yvonne fits in here like a hand in a glove, keeping the character and traditions of the place alive—which the undead really appreciate!

But you don't have to simply take my word for it. Yvonne opens her home every Christmas season during Montgomery's holiday house tours. (And FYI, her house is the only one on the tour to serve alcohol!) Standing by the warmth of the fire in the tavern room, sipping a glass of spirits, in the company of good friends, I think you will find that the timeline between past and present will blur, and you will feel the hospitality of centuries gone by. History is alive here, even if most of the former occupants are not!

Butchered and Burned?
Sullivan County, NY

I love searching through old newspapers to look for ghost stories. While going through some archives of Sullivan County, New York newspapers I came upon the following article from February 26, 1903, which certainly caught my attention.

Thrilling Tales Told of Murdered Man's Home

The Centreville correspondent of the Middletown press writes that the surreptitiously inclined residents of that locality firmly believe that the house where "Lafe" Taylor was so brutally murdered by his wife is haunted.

He states that all sorts of blood curdling ghost and hobgoblin stories are in circulation, and according to the village stove committee anyone who might be skeptical on the matter may have the truth of the story firmly impressed upon his mind by a visit on any night just after midnight to the lonesome spot where the Taylor abode is located, and he will certainly hear the agonizing cries of distress which emanate nightly from the shanty where "Lafe" Taylor and his "butcher" spouse made their home.

The Liberty Herald is informed that the Taylor house, where the recent murder was committed, is being torn to pieces by curious people who want pieces of it for souvenirs. A Liberty photographer who visited the house says that when he saw the outside of it, he concluded that he would as soon be murdered as to live there. After viewing the inside he decided that if he had to live there, he would insist on being murdered.

As old newspapers are notorious for sensationalizing crimes–and come to think of it, so are our modern newspapers–I needed to find out the details of this particular murder and if the nature of the crime could have lead to the alleged haunted activity. While the article referred to the victim's wife as a "butcher," I knew better than to take that at face value. For all I knew, the man had been stabbed with a pen knife and the local journalist took poetic license in exaggerating the facts.

Was I ever surprised when I found out the truth! After tracking down and reading about a dozen articles on the case, I can state with absolute certainty that if anyone ever deserved the title of butcher, it was Mrs. Kate Taylor. But let me give you the details of this gruesome murder as it unfolded to the public.

It was in early February of 1903 when Lafayette Taylor did not show up for a job and people began wondering where he was. When asked, his wife said he had gone to Orange County looking for work and had never returned. As there had been considerable turmoil in the marriage–and that is a great understatement, as I will explain shortly–it wasn't surprising to anyone that "Lafe," as he was known, could have run out on his wife and 14-year-old stepdaughter, Ida May DeKay. However, the potentially perfect crime aroused suspicion when Kate made an unusual declaration.

She tried to sell Lafe's horse to a man in town, but the man was afraid that Lafe would return and demand his horse be given back to him. As Lafe was well known to be a violent and abusive drunk, the man did not want to risk buying the horse, even at a bargain price. Insistent that he purchase the animal, Kate said the oddest thing to "reassure" him. She told the man not to worry about Lafe returning, because she had killed him, and then cut up his body into little pieces and burned them!

It seemed impossible to believe, but the man went to the authorities just in the case there was a one in a million chance Kate was telling the truth about murdering her husband. Kate's daughter, Ida, was brought in for questioning, and at first was reluctant to speak against her mother. That reluctance quickly vanished, however, when she was offered the sum of five dollars to testify against her mother!

Yet, even when she confirmed that Kate had killed Lafayette, and she then helped her mother butcher and burn the body, the district attorney could not believe the girl's story. How could anyone believe that a wife and young girl could do such a hideous and barbaric thing!?

DISTRICT ATTORNEY DOUBTS IDA TAYLOR'S STORY.

It is understood that District Attorney Anderson and those interested with him in securing all the evidence in the Lafayette Taylor murder case do not believe that all the body of the murdered man was burned by Mrs. Taylor.

An article in the local paper spoke to the belief that Lafe had indeed been murdered, and the extreme lengths his friends were taking in the search for his body:

A Middletown clairvoyant has been employed by the friends of the late "Lafe" Taylor to locate his body, the friends doubting the story of his daughter who said her mother chopped up the body and burned it in the stove. The clairvoyant says she knows what disposition was made of the body, but will not tell until properly compensated for her time and services.

Authorities were taking a more conservative route, believing that Kate must have simply disposed of her husband's body in a local lake. Although the lake had several feet of ice on it, there was one section where some ice had been cut and removed. The surface had refrozen there, but only to a depth of a few inches. The District Attorney ordered that section of ice cut away, and the bottom of the lake dredged, but found nothing. Unable to locate Taylor's body anywhere, authorities were forced to reexamine Kate's original confession, and Ida's story. There is that old saying that when all other possibilities can be dismissed, the one remaining, however unlikely, has to be the truth—and that truth was truly horrific.

During the trial of Kate Taylor, her daughter Ida gave a detailed and chilling account of the events of that night. While her mother had claimed that Lafe had come home drunk and had started to beat her, Ida claimed that the couple was quietly drinking tea at the dining table when she went to bed. The next thing she knew, she was awakened by the sound of gunshots.

Hurrying to the kitchen, Ida stated that she found her mother chopping off Lafayette's head and arm with an ax. The girl then helped cut up the body up with that ax, storing the pieces in a basin in the pantry. Over the course of several days, they would put a few more chunks into the wood stove to burn the flesh and bones. The ashes and some of the smaller bones were ground up and then mixed with the chicken feed, and subsequently devoured. The larger bones were scorched, but not easy to grind, so they were buried beneath a manure pile.

Ida even claimed that the morning after the murder, having just burned her husband's head and arm in the stove, Kate Taylor calmly made pancakes for breakfast on that very same stove! She went on to explain to the shocked jurors that wallpaper was used to cover the bullet holes, and a fresh coat of paint hid all the blood stains.

> **MRS. LAFAYETTE TAYLOR MURDERED HER HUSBAND**
>
> **AND BURNED HIS BODY IN A COOK STOVE.**
>
> **WOMAN HAS CONFESSED AND IS IN JAIL.**

Kate claimed that her actions were in self-defense, but stories emerged that she had already tried to murder her husband once before. While Lafe had been sleeping in the barn, Kate boarded the door and set fire to the building! In her defense, friends of Kate testified that they had witnessed Lafe regularly beating and abusing his wife, often knocking her to the floor. As part of the prosecution, friends of Lafe stated that he had numerous scars where Kate had beaten *him* with an ax handle!

> **HOW MRS. TAYLOR KILLED AND BURNED HER HUSBAND.**
>
> **FIRST SHOT HIM AND THEN CUT OFF HIS HEAD.**
>
> **TESTIMONY WHICH IMPRESSED THE JURY.**

The plot thickened even more when another man entered the legal scene. Local farmer Peter Yerkin was arrested and accused of not only being Kate's lover, but her co-conspirator. Some claimed that Yerkin had even been the driving force behind the murder, hounding Kate until she finally did his dirty work for him.

Kate went on the record in saying that someone else had been involved in the murder, although she didn't specifically name Yerkin. A neighbor testified that Yerkin knew all of the details of the murder before anyone else, and that Yerkin had threatened to do him harm if he told anyone about his involvement in the crime. Yet, loyal friends swore that Yerkin was a quiet, simple farmer who had been falsely accused.

Newspaper accounts described Yerkin as an emotional and physical wreck behind bars, breaking under the strain of his imprisonment and all the interrogations. While the rumor mill had no doubt of his guilt, ultimately, no substantial evidence could be produced, and Yerkin was set free. I found a reference in a newspaper article some years later that reported that Yerkin had gotten married, so apparently he was able to get his life back in order.

> Peter Yerkins, who is in Monticello jail, awaiting the action of the grand jury, on a charge of being an accessory to the murder of Lafayette Taylor, is said to be breaking down under the strain and weeps much of the time. Mrs. Taylor's jail life apparently agrees with her.

Was Yerkin guilty, or innocent? I suspect he at least had prior knowledge of the crime, and perhaps some involvement. Ida had apparently said that right after the murder, her mother opened the front door and swung a lantern back and forth, as if signaling someone that the deed had been done. Of course, suspicions are one thing, and proof in a court of law is entirely different, so Yerkin was released.

Not so for Mrs. Kate Taylor, who was convicted of first degree murder, sentenced to death, and sent to prison in Dannemora, New York, on June 2 (made famous in 2015 by the two prisoners who made a daring escape and were on the run for three weeks). She was to die in the electric chair the week of July 5, but within just a few days of being executed, she was granted a second trial. This time she was only found guilty of second degree murder, and sent to the Matteawan State Hospital for the Criminally Insane in Fishkill, New York. Although spared from execution, her health quickly deteriorated, and Kate Taylor died in prison in 1907.

Ida was never charged with any crime, even though she was clearly an accessory after the fact. Not too many 14-year-old girls would have the intestinal fortitude to help cut up and burn their stepfather, and she never seems to have had any remorse for her actions, or sympathy for the victim. If Lafe was an abusive drunk, Ida was probably happy to see him go. And if authorities hadn't given her $5 to testify, who knows if the crime would ever have been solved!

While this all seems like the script for a pulp fiction novel, one real question remains—was the house haunted by the ghost of the murdered, butchered, and burned Lafe Taylor? According to the terrified locals, they had no doubt. I know it all sounds too fantastic, and a great exaggeration. But then again, initially, so did the story of a woman who shot her husband, cut him into little pieces, burned his flesh and bones, and fed the ashes to the chickens…

St. John's-in-the-Wilderness
Stony Point, NY

At first thought, churches would appear to be among the least likely places to be haunted. However, upon further consideration, one realizes that there are deep, spiritual attachments people form to their places of worship during their lives—attachments which may carry over to death. Then there is the 800-pound paranormal gorilla in the room—many churches have cemeteries, which are prime real estate for wandering spirits.

On April 25, 2015, I was fortunate enough to give one of my ghost lectures on the property of St. John's-in-the-Wilderness, in the town of Stony Point, New York. The name is appropriate, as this beautiful old stone church, built in 1880, is the only privately owned land in the midst of the vast 44,000 acres of Harriman State Park. The funding for the church came from Mrs. Margaret Furniss Zimmerman, in memory of her husband, John, who choked to death on their honeymoon in Egypt. (There are conflicting accounts of him choking on a cherry pit or pomegranate seeds in either Egypt or Palestine.)

The Furniss family of Portsmouth, New Hampshire, had made their fortunes in trade with the West Indies. Although Margaret had five brothers, none of them had "a head for business" and their incompetence and dissolute lifestyles lead their father to cutting them all out of his will.

Instead, he left his entire $50 million estate to his daughter Margaret and her two sisters in 1871, which was a remarkable thing to do for the time.

At this point in her life, Margaret was already well into spinsterhood at the age of 43. However, within a year of her father's death—and her enormous inheritance—she finally married 41-year-old John Edward Zimmerman on June 4, 1872. John was the Vice Consul of the Netherlands in New York City, and had known Margaret for many decades. I may be cynical, but I suspect that Margaret did not become attractive enough to marry until she had her share of the $50,000,000 in her bank account.

Even if John had married her for her money, Margaret genuinely seemed to love her husband. She never remarried, and she donated the land and money to build a church in John's memory. In addition to the church, there was also a school and an orphanage. The grieving widow's charitable practices were greatly helped by another woman, Ada Bessie Carey, a teacher in Tomkin's Cove, but originally from the Isle of Guernsey, in the English Channel. (The history of these two women and their work at the church has been detailed in Odessa Elliott's book *That Much Good Might Be Done*.)

My lecture that night was in the former barn across the street from the church. There was a blazing fire in the fireplace, and a good crowd of people to whom I told some of my favorite ghost stories. And what better way to end the night for my husband Bob Strong, and I, than with a tour/ghost hunt of the church itself? The church's Senior Warden,

Charles McCartney, lead the way, and we were also accompanied by his wife Paule, and church members Barbara Sikorsky, Kasey Sikorsky, Brandy Collishaw, and Jennifer Collishaw.

Charles has lived in the house across the street from the church since 2012, and he has seen and experienced some remarkable things. His dog gets him up "at all hours," and one night while he was out clearing some snow for the dog, he saw something in the road. There is only one streetlight in that isolated area, and by that light he saw someone walking down the street along the cemetery. That was unusual enough considering the location, weather, and time of night, but this visitor went at least a step or two beyond bizarre, as only his legs were visible from the knees down! These disembodied legs even cast a shadow from the streetlight!

Charles was understandably stunned by the legs, which disappeared as suddenly as they had appeared. It was so strange, that he never even told his wife or anyone else about them. So imagine his shock, when one day Kasey Sikorski recounted a story her brother had told her. About ten years earlier, he also saw a pair of legs, just from the knees down, walking by that cemetery!

Who can say why these legs wander this street by the cemetery, but Charles reminded me that there had been a plane crash nearby. In 1974, Northwest Orient Airlines Flight 6231 had been chartered to pick up the

Baltimore Colts football team in Buffalo on December 1, 1974. It was a bitter cold night, and icing led to the fatal crash of the Boeing 727, killing the crew of three. Even 40 years later, pieces of the wreckage are still scattered around the site. Could the victims—or at least pieces of them—still be seen to this day, as well?

Another startling incident occurred about 8am one Sunday morning as Charles was getting the church ready for services. The vacuum cleaner cord reaches about halfway down the aisle from the altar, and as he was changing the location of the plug to do the other half of the church, he turned and saw a woman sitting in a pew.

"She looked completely real and solid, with brown hair, and wearing old-fashioned clothes with a high white collar," Charles explained. "I said, 'Whoa!' and then she was gone. She looked like the woman in the stained glass window."

The window to which he is referring depicts the patroness of the church, Margaret Furniss Zimmerman. She passed away in 1918, but perhaps she still visits the place into which she poured her heart and money for so many years.

The most common occurrence takes place in Charles' office–or to be more accurate, in the orphanage room directly above his office where the sounds of footsteps are quite common. Wondering if he was imagining things, Charles was relieved the day his wife was doing some work in that office.

"How did you make out over there?" he asked Paule when she came home.

"Fine," she replied, but then continued with a puzzled look, "but who was that walking around upstairs?"

Most recently, when Charles was closing up after an event at the church, he found that a light was still on in an upstairs bathroom. As he was walking towards the stairs, he heard a whistle; the familiar two notes one uses to try to get someone's attention. Ignoring the distinctive sound, he continued upstairs and heard the whistle again, which was louder and more insistent this time. The third time he heard the whistle, he said out loud, "Leave me alone, I don't have time for this!"

Immediately, the toilet flushed! Clearly someone wanted his attention, or perhaps was trying to freak him out just a little bit for fun. Was it a prank from one of the former occupants of the orphanage?

"That toilet had never flushed on its own before," Charles replied to my question about the plumbing. "And it has never done that since."

A more unnerving event took place late one warm evening when Charles was walking his dog on the road. He could hear rhythmic sounds rising up from the cemetery.

"Wait a minute, that's not frogs," he said to himself. "It's chanting!"

Were some drunken kids playing a joke, or was a strange cult conducting some sort of ritual in the cemetery? Determined to find out, Charles continued down the hill where the sound of chanting intensified. Sweeping the area with his bright flashlight, fully expecting to see a group of people, he instead saw nothing but tombstones, and when he reached the bottom of the hill, the chanting stopped and there was silence. He waited for a few moments, but heard and saw nothing, so he decided to return home. The moment he started to walk back up the hill, however, the chanting started again! He did not return for a second look.

Additionally, Charles and other witnesses have experienced the following:

- Someone coughing when no one else is there
- Knocking sounds on a tree in the cemetery
- A little black dog running around the cemetery
- Organ music playing when the church is empty
- Doors opening and closing on their own
- Feeling of a presence and being watched

Our ghost hunt began by entering the front door of the old church. It has a beautiful interior and we admired the stained glass windows as best we could in the dark. We decided to concentrate on the most active part of the building complex, the orphanage, and it wasn't long before I realized why the place had such a reputation. We were all in the one large bedroom of the former orphanage when we heard some type of rumbling somewhere in the building, and a soft tapping sound out in the hall. I asked Charles about the heating system and he informed me that all of the boilers were shut off, so they could not be the source of the rumbling sounds. Clear and distinct footsteps out in the hallway further convinced me that what we were hearing had nothing to do with the structure's pipes.

To help triangulate the sounds, I went toward the bathroom in the middle of the hallway while everyone else remained in the bedroom. On the audio recording, I report that there is definitely "movement in the house" and "loud footsteps" although it was hard to place its exact location. For a time, these footsteps and sounds could be heard in the hallway, staircase, and whatever room we were *not* in –as if someone was playing games with us and just remaining out of reach. But then it got rather intense as we all gathered back in the orphanage bedroom.

The orphanage room.

Jennifer suddenly found it hard to breathe and saw a seven or eight year old blond boy sitting in a chair. Brandy felt her arm being touched and brushed by a cold hand and felt somewhat unbalanced. Later, both women explained that they had young children, so perhaps they were singled out because the spirits of the former orphans saw them as mother figures. We stayed for quite a while in that room and the signs of paranormal activity were numerous and quite obvious. Anyone with any degree of sensitivity would be in for a wild night if they tried to sleep here!

We went downstairs and Charles, Bob, Brandy and I decided to go down into the basement while the others remained on the first floor above us. I examined the well and could see the water inside and spoke to Charles about how wells in houses often seemed to be focal points for unusual activity. As his office was just above the well and below the orphanage bedroom, I described his workplace as a "paranormal sandwich."

As we stood quietly in the dark and cramped old basement, there were footsteps going back and forth over our heads, even though we had requested the others to stay still and remain quiet.

"Okay, they must be moving around upstairs," I concluded, a little disappointed that the others had disregarded our request.

Shortly after, we heard tapping on the floor above our heads and we once again assumed that it was the other members of our group. About the same time, Brandy once again felt someone touching her hair. We remained for a while longer but as the footsteps and tapping above us persisted, we decided it was pointless to try to conduct a quiet investigation. However, we were about to be quite surprised when we went back upstairs.

"*We sat still! We didn't move!*" both Barbara and Kasey emphatically insisted when I asked them about all the noise. They then turned the tables and asked us if *we* had been making the scratching sounds on the basement door.

From the sounds they were hearing on the first floor above us, they assumed Charles had come back upstairs and for some reason was scratching on the door. It took a few moments to sort things out, but it quickly became clear that the footsteps and tapping we were hearing in the basement and the scratching sounds they were hearing on the first floor were not created by any of the living there that night!

"OK, that's pretty good. I'm impressed," I stated, once I realized what had really been going on during that part of the investigation.

And it was even more fascinating that we had not heard any of the scratching sounds, while they had not heard any of the footsteps and tapping which should have been occurring right in front of them on that first floor. It was all really amazing activity, but nothing compared to what I was about to experience.

We went back to the church and while everyone chose a pew and sat down, I moved around with my EMF meter. I didn't find any unusual readings, but while I was near the altar, something extraordinary happened

–something to this day I still can't explain. I had turned to face the pews and Brandy was standing near the organ, when I asked for a sign of the presence of any spirits in the church. Suddenly, there was an odd rushing sound that started out faintly, but quickly grew in intensity.

It's difficult to describe, but it was like a combination of a strong gust of wind and the sound of many people suddenly running, like a stampede. I had time to ask out loud, "What is that," thinking it had to be something with the building as it was growing so loud, but then I couldn't speak, as the growing sound was suddenly unleashed and rushed straight for me. I instinctively put up my hands as if to block people from running into me, but of course, no one was physically there. I think I gasped in surprise as this rush of sound swept over me, passed the altar to the back wall of the church, where it actually then *went up the wall* before it fell silent. I just stood there stunned for a few seconds, trying to comprehend what had just happened

None of the others sitting in the pews had heard the rushing sound, but fortunately, Brandy had been close enough to hear it, and she also described it as the sound of many running feet. I immediately had to exit the church and go around to the back to see if somehow I had mistaken that rushing sound, and maybe it had simply been the wind blowing tree branches back and forth against the back wall making an awful scraping sound. But what I found was that there wasn't a tree within 100 feet of the back of the church, and the wall was made of solid stone, so it would have been very hard to produce any kind of sounds inside of the church.

So what had it been? What had rushed past me when I asked for a sign? Had all the lost souls of Saint John's-in-the-Wilderness Church gathered and swept over me to convince me of their presence? If so, I am convinced! In my 20 years of ghost hunting, I never heard anything like that sound. And I feel both fortunate, and a little freaked out, to have experienced it.

Buyer Beware
Ulster County, NY

There were footsteps in the house, and an inexplicable and unnerving banging sound coming from the kitchen. Rachel and Tara had only recently moved in, and as Rachel worked long hours, often at night, Tara was the one who experienced the brunt of this paranormal activity. No one had told them about the place before they purchased it, which was unfortunate, as it was harboring a very deep, dark secret.

The neighbors had heard that banging sound before. About six months earlier, they thought the owner, "John," was on a drunken rampage and was punching and kicking the walls of his home. In fact, he was kicking the kitchen wall—in his final death struggle, as he hung suspended by his neck from a rope he had tied to a beam in the ceiling. This tragic suicide has not only left its mark in the minds of the neighbors, it has also left a terrible imprint on the house, as well as leaving John's angry, restless, and remorseful spirit to torment the living.

I became acquainted with this case through psychic Barbara Bleitzhofer, who told me that one day Rachel and Tara showed up at her house looking for her help. They lived just a few blocks away and had heard of Barbara's amazing abilities. Rachel explained that while she had experienced a few things—such as being growled at—the activity at their house didn't really bother her.

However, Tara was another story; she was quite concerned by the noises, the dark shadowy figures, and the overwhelming presence of John, who even appeared in her bedroom several times! In addition, Tara had experienced "frigid chills," terrible pains, had seen lights go on and off by themselves, and a door opening by itself. They were desperate to stop all of this activity and bring some peace to their home.

Barbara arranged to come by the following week with Duane Smith. Barb recorded the entire session for me as I was unable to be there, and she admitted on the audio recording to feeling a little nervous as they approached the house one Saturday morning in May, 2015. They all stood in the yard for a few minutes talking in general about the activity.

As I listened to the audio recording few weeks later, I noticed some very loud banging sounds in the background, like sharp hammering, or perhaps even gunshots. I immediately contacted Barbara to see if someone was target shooting, or if there was any construction in the neighborhood, but she indicated that there was no one shooting or any work that she knew of taking place nearby.

Barb and Duane had not yet listened to the audio recording, but when they did, they both agreed that no one had heard those sounds at the time, which is quite amazing. How could a long series of loud, sharp, banging sounds nearby go unnoticed by four people standing in a quiet yard, yet be recorded? Could that digital recorder have captured the sounds of John's death struggle?

Rachel and Tara explained that the activity was at its worst when they first moved in, but it strangely began to subside after they made a particular purchase. They had bought and installed a wood pellet stove, which helped make the house warm and cozy. This may seem like an odd thing to pacify a spirit, until you understand the nature of the suicide.

John's life had spiraled out of control over the course of a year or two. His drug and alcohol addictions had led to him losing his wife and children. Then he found out he was seriously ill with a deadly form of cancer. He lost his job and when his money ran out, his utilities were cut off. The last straw came that bitter winter's day when he was forced to remove his wood stove, as it was not up to the safety codes, leaving him with no heat, no light, and no hope. The removal of that wood stove had left an exposed beam in the kitchen ceiling—the same beam where he tied that rope, made a noose, and ended his young life.

So when Rachel and Tara installed the pellet stove, perhaps it figuratively warmed and soothed John's cold and agitated spirit. Unfortunately, however, it did not completely end the activity. After Tara spent many long hours afraid and alone in the house, they decided to seek Barbara's help.

I felt as if I was with Barbara and Duane as I listened to the audio recordings. As soon as they entered the house, Barb said she was having trouble breathing, as her throat felt constricted.

"I'm shaking really bad, Linda," she said, knowing I would want a minute-by-minute account of their experiences. "He had a lot of problems, and his mind was altered by booze, drugs, and his illness."

Duane also felt the heaviness of the atmosphere, as well as finding it hard to breathe.

"I'm feeling very emotional," Duane explained "Almost like crying."

This photo says it all as Barbara communicates with John's agitated spirit in the kitchen where he committed suicide.   Photo courtesy of Duane Smith.

Barbara felt that John had *not* intentionally killed himself, and that it wasn't something he had planned to do. She believed he was in a daze from drugs and alcohol, and only realized at the last moment what he was doing, and started kicking and thrashing to try to save himself. The circumstances of the case may bear this out, as when his friend came looking for him, he thought that John was just standing in the corner of his kitchen.

Only upon closer inspection, did he realize that John was dead, and hanging just an inch or two above of the floor! In fact, John was so low that the tips of his toes were able to touch the floor, so he had obviously not initiated the act with a clear mind, or fatal intent, or he would have made the rope much shorter.

If true, this makes the suicide all the more tragic, and leaves John with an even greater level of regret and anger. He is anxious to take back what he has done–which, of course, is now impossible, as this swirl of negative emotions keeps him locked to the location of his death. I have said this many times over the years: people who commit suicide have no idea of the effect they have on not only their family and friends, but also on the lives of people they inadvertently cause to suffer, simply because those people now inhabit the space where someone took his or her own life.

Barbara spent a considerable amount of time trying to talk to John and get him to release his negativity and move on. It was not an easy task–it never is in such cases–but when Rachel and Tara both expressed their sympathy for what John had to endure in life, his attitude appeared to soften.

"He is sending you red hearts," Barbara told the two women. "I haven't seen that before. There is now a ray of hope for him."

Barbara urged John to go to the light, but she heard him reply he was "not a carnival act," although she felt it was more of a display of his sense of humor than a statement of defiance. At least they had opened a dialogue and let John know that he was not alone, that people *did* care about him.

And in death, as in life, isn't that all we really need?

Note: I regret to report that soon after this story was written, Tara moved out of the house.

Gone, But Never Forgotten
Warwick, NY

"It must have been a chupacabra," César's husband joked to lighten the mood.

However, the attack was no laughing matter. It was a hot, summer day around 2005, and either a Thursday or Friday. César was in the side yard of their 232-year-old home in Warwick, New York, looking for their cat around 7pm. There was no wind, and it was very quiet–in fact, unnaturally quiet–considering the usual traffic on Route 17A, and the noise from the community pool in the housing development on the adjacent property.

Due to the heat, César was not wearing a shirt. Usually, all one would have to worry about would be some mosquito bites, or perhaps the sting of a bee. However, what happened was clearly not the result of any insect.

"I suddenly got a chill," César explained, "and I was afraid to turn around because I felt like someone was there. I just kept walking, and then I felt a large hand touching my back, but I just kept walking and wouldn't turn around to look. It was just so strange that everything was so silent, when there were usually so many sounds. I don't know what it was, but I just kept walking and went back to the house."

The next morning, his husband looked at César's back and saw long, angry scratches from six or seven fingers! Whatever had made them, had to have been a very large animal—or person. To make it even more bizarre, César did not feel any pain when it happened, just the touch of a hand. Even when the scratches were healing there was no pain, irritation, or itching, and the marks eventually faded and went away. However, the memory of the event has not faded.

On another occasion, César was sitting on the back porch. About 40 or 50 yards away, something caught his eye. It was a man walking; a very tall man, but unlike anyone he had ever seen.

"It was a watery image," he explained, or at least tried to with something that appears to defy explanation. "It was shaped like a man and walking like a man, but it was just this rippling, watery image, and it was very, very tall."

Needless to say, these two experiences made him feel somewhat uncomfortable about being out in the yard alone, especially at night. He used to go out at all hours to sit on the porch, but no longer, at least not by himself. At this location, however, going indoors may be even more of an adventure, as over the years he has heard noises and voices, and has seen shadows, as well as things that are far more defined.

For example, one day when he was in the bathroom with the door open, he saw the figure of a soldier pointing his rifle at him. Unnerving enough, to be sure, but this figure went beyond even the "normal" paranormal.

"It reminded me of one of those green plastic soldiers," César told me, "only this one was clear. He was completely transparent!"

About a week after their beloved cat died, César said he heard what sounded like his husband crying in the house. He called out to him, but got no response. He followed the sound of the very emotional sobbing to the living room, where he expected to find his husband in tears because of the loss of their cat, but he found no one and the sound had stopped. He searched the house to no avail, and when he got to the kitchen and looked out, he saw that his husband was in the garden, weeding. He went out and spoke to him and confirmed that his husband had not been in the house recently, so where had the heartfelt weeping come from?

"It was such an intensely emotional time. It was like the house had recorded the sounds of my husband crying, because it sounded exactly like him. I think this house holds the impressions of events," César explained, trying to make sense of the many odd things that have happened here.

More evidence of this was to come after his husband unfortunately passed away in the fall of 2014, after a long illness. About three or four weeks later, César heard a voice crying out in distress. A week after that, he felt someone grab his elbow. Around the same time, César was trying to locate the set of master keys to the house. He looked everywhere and was ready to give up, when one day he returned from visiting his husband's grave, when he noticed that some boxes by the staircase had been moved.

"I had no idea how those boxes could have moved, but I decided to look inside one of them. "I reached in and felt a stack of papers and letters, and then I heard a very distinctive noise. Under those papers was the set of keys! I felt it was my husband helping me and I thanked him out loud for showing me where the keys were, as I never would have found them on my own."

Then there was the time he was sweeping the floor and bent down with the dust pan. About nine feet away he saw a male standing there, wearing "pistachio-colored clothes." Another time, he saw a more conservatively dressed man in blue in the backyard.

With so much occurring over the span of so many years, I had to ask if all this activity he had experienced occurred only at this location, or had he been experiencing such things his entire life? César told me that when he was growing up Mexico, many strange things happened. He was particularly adept at knowing when someone was going to die. A thought or image of a person would suddenly come to him, and "within two or three days I would hear about that person's death."

I have often found that houses with a lot of unusual activity draw people who are very sensitive. It is like some form of mutual attraction that such places often get new owners who have the ability to see and hear the spirits that wander there. Which isn't to say that this is a good situation–such sensitive people don't always feel comfortable in their own homes, and I still firmly believe that spirits have better places to move on to than the places they use to live, or where their deaths or other tragedies occurred.

Naturally, after speaking with César and hearing his fascinating stories, I had to experience the house and property myself, or at the very least, see where his experiences occurred to get a better perspective. And who better to do that with than my very talented psychic friend, Barbara Bleitzhofer?

It was a very cool and rainy day in early June of 2015 when I pulled into the driveway of the historic home in Warwick. Not too many places have one of those official blue and yellow plaques standing in their front yards, so my first action was to take a picture of it.

The Sayer family owned large pieces of property in Warwick—enough so that they were able to donate the land for the county park across the street.

César greeted me at the door, and my initial impressions were that this was a charming and elegant home, with a marvelous collection of artwork—the type of place I would pay to stay in when on vacation! We sat in the parlor for a few minutes before Barbara arrived, along with Duane Smith, who would once again help by taking photos. It would have been nice to linger on the couch for a little while chatting, but images and voices were already coming to Barbara fast and furious, so we got right down to work.

"There's a woman," she began. "And this woman was the queen of the house. This was *hers*, this was *hers*, she keeps saying."

Barb went on to describe this woman wearing fancy dresses and entertaining on a grand scale, with many influential people attending these soirees. I asked César if he knew any family history about the people who lived here, and he had something even better—photographs.

"That's her! She is still here," Barbara said with certainty, as she pointed to a beautiful young woman in early 20th century clothing standing in front of the house, whom César identified as Molly Sayer.

He explained that Molly left the house around 1958, and died in Florida in the 1990s.

"I'm surprised she came back here," César said.

At that moment my EMF meter lit up like a Christmas tree.

"She definitely came back," Barb said, without a doubt. "She was very happy here."

We discussed Molly for a few more minutes, with the EMF meter going off several more times at key moments, like when discussing her death.

We then walked through the library and the living room, where Barb felt strong female energies. However, the dining room was all male, and César explained that in earlier days, this room had a bar and a pool table, so this definitely was where the men of the house congregated. Overall, these rooms were full of positive feelings from spirits who enjoyed their time in this house.

Barbara and César discuss the energies attached to
some of the paintings in the dining room, which may add
to the overall activity in the house.

Not so, back by the kitchen and the room next to it. We all felt a heaviness and sadness, and Barb said this room "needed to be opened up to release all that sad energy." This all made perfect sense when we found out this this was the sick room where César's husband spent his last days and passed away just several months earlier. Despite the love they had between them, the sorrow of death does leave a thick residue. Fresh air, sunlight, and laughter can help dissipate and release that heaviness.

One of the upstairs bedrooms had a very calming, relaxing feeling. As Barb was describing the older woman and younger man who used to stay here over the years as guests, our EMF meters lit up.

This was all fascinating, but from the time Barbara arrived, I could tell she was holding back something. Finally, in this room, she couldn't hold back any longer.

"I don't want to upset you," she began gently, looking at César, "but your husband is still with you all the time."

César expressed the same sentiment and told Barbara he had no problem speaking about him. She was visibly relieved to hear that, as the man's presence had been so strong and persistent. She also said that his spirit was delighted that we were here doing this, and he wanted Barb to give César a "big hug." At that moment our EMF meters lit up again, and we were all covered in goose bumps!

When we entered the next bedroom, I felt quite a surge of energy and my EMF meter went off again and again. I described the room as "electric." Barb got a "grandma vibe," but I said I got a much more energetic sensation. I strongly felt that there was something that should be done in here. The readings were highest by the bed, and it was there that a collection of artwork was sitting in a large pile.

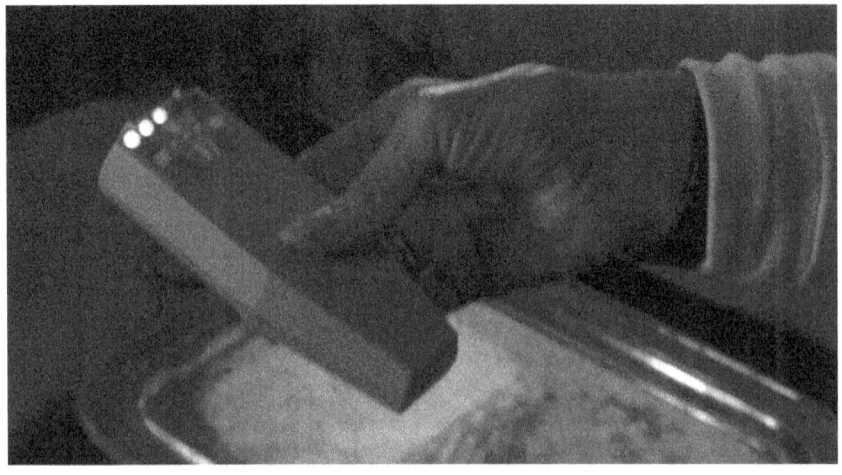

Duane took this photo of my EMF meter lighting up by the artwork.

César told us that the artist passed away around 1970, and while he never met her, he kept thinking about her after he discovered the box filled with her work. After a while, he decided to go through the contents of the box and realized that the paintings, which were mostly water colors, had been untouched for 45 years and were in mint condition. He now wants to make her life's work known, and plans on contacting galleries in Connecticut, where many of her scenes were painted, to see if they might hold an exhibit.

I can't tell you how excited and happy this made *me* feel—although I know I was just experiencing the joy that *she* was feeling. This woman is still very much attached to her work, and if César can bring it to the attention of the world, there is no better gift he could give her. What artist wouldn't want people to see and appreciate their beloved creations?

"She *is* the energy in the room!" I stated, as the electricity in the room increased. "I think she very much wants you to do this."

I am visibly excited and happy to know that this artist's work will get recognition. (Photo courtesy of Duane Smith.)

We continued on through the other various rooms of the house, including the attic and basement, and Barb talked about all the spirits and energies connected to both the rooms and the antique furniture. Nothing was threatening or overwhelming, but after I listened to the audio recordings, I fully realized just how active this place is! For those who are receptive, it is a carnival for the senses.

Barbara feels a strong presence from the artist's self-portrait.

We then went out into the yard, in between downpours, and in the area where César had seen the watery figure, Barb felt there was something like a portal located there. As a spirit passes through worlds, it could appear to be rippling, like a heat wave or a watery form. She felt that what César saw, originated from a very long time ago.

César describes to Barbara the watery figure he witnessed as they stand in the portal area of the yard.

Barbara also felt the presence of many soldiers from around the time of the Revolutionary War. That made perfect sense, as not only was Captain Daniel Sayer a soldier living in a military blockhouse on this property, but just down the road I had seen an historic marker that indicated that the 3rd New Hampshire Regiment was camped there during the Revolutionary War.

We then went over to the area of the yard where César had been scratched. Barbara felt very strange there, and thought that perhaps there may be something under the ground, like old tunnels. When César described his eerie encounter on this spot, Barb shook her head and said it *wasn't a human spirit* that did that. What it was, she couldn't say, but that certainly opened up even more bizarre possibilities!

Barbara and I reluctantly stand on the spot where César was scratched.

All in all, this old Warwick house is a fascinating place with a wide variety of activity and spirits. Five generations of the Sayers lived and died here, and so it would not be surprising if Molly Sayer or other family members still resided in the place that held so many memories for them. Then there are all the antiques and paintings that contribute their own unique energies into the mix. And as if all of this paranormal activity inside the house wasn't enough, the property may contain portals to other worlds—some of which may be inhuman!

Last, and by no means least, is the bond of love that still exists between César and his recently departed husband—although he has departed only in the physical sense.

We discussed all of this in the dining room after the investigation. César was kind enough to warm our chilled bones with some wonderful homemade tea and pastries, served with a silver teapot and fine china. I joked that he was spoiling us and we weren't used to such good treatment in such beautiful surroundings. At the same time, however, I was thinking of how lucky César and his husband had been to find one another, and to spend all those happy years together in this wonderful home.

This is a ghost story in the technical sense, but I also view this as a love story—the love a family has for their ancestral home, the love an artist has for her work, and the love that not even death can vanquish.

Montgomery Firehouse
Montgomery, NY

In September of 2014, I was contacted by Robin from the Montgomery Fire Department. We had met a couple of times at the Wallkill River School (a.k.a. the Patchett House) in Montgomery during my Halloween lectures and ghost tours. She told me that the firehouse had a history of activity, including some very recent events. Intrigued, we arranged an investigation a couple of weeks later. Fortunately, Barbara Bleitzhofer and Duane Smith were also on board.

When I arrived that evening, Barbara and Duane were already there and appeared to be watching something behind the firehouse. I got out of the car and saw that some sort of party was underway, which turned out to be a wedding reception—but not your typical wedding reception, as they had a mechanical bull!

In any event, we went inside and met with Robin and Mike, who has been with the Montgomery fire department for 26 years. Mike surprised us by saying that there had been a sighting just the night before. One of the members had fallen asleep on a couch, and when he woke up, he saw someone standing by the door, who then just disappeared. But I would hear more about that when the witness, himself, arrived later on.

"Generally, everything centers around the room we're in," Mike said, as we sat in the Members' Room, "which is in the dead center of the firehouse. Through that glass window, numerous people, including myself, have seen somebody walk by, and you go running out there to see who it is, and there's nobody there. Or, you're standing somewhere in the vicinity and you'll hear the front door open, then we walk over to see who's in the building, and there's nobody there.

The Members' Room

"Ten or twelve years ago, we thought someone was sleeping in here so we pulled a 'sting' at three o'clock in the morning. There were twenty of us, and we hit every door in the firehouse simultaneously, because we really thought someone was sleeping here somewhere. But no. No one.

"So this has just been going on and on, and it's mostly the shadows, and it's centered around this room. It's in the bays there, and this room. When you see them, you're not paying attention, you're watching TV or reading a book, and you see someone walk by and wonder who it could be."

"And the automated lights come on, and the PASS alarm," Robin added.

I asked what a PASS alarm was, and Mike explained it was a safety device hooked into a fireman's breathing apparatus. PASS stands for Personal Alert Safety System, and these units begin to sound an alarm if a firefighter has not moved for 30 seconds, and the alarm increases in intensity if he or she remains motionless. By regulation, such units must produce at least 95 decibels of deafening sound, to help rescuers locate their fallen comrade in distress. They are not supposed to go off on their own when not in use and sitting in a fire truck, but that is exactly what happened. I was to find out greater detail about this incident later, when I interviewed one of the men who witnessed it.

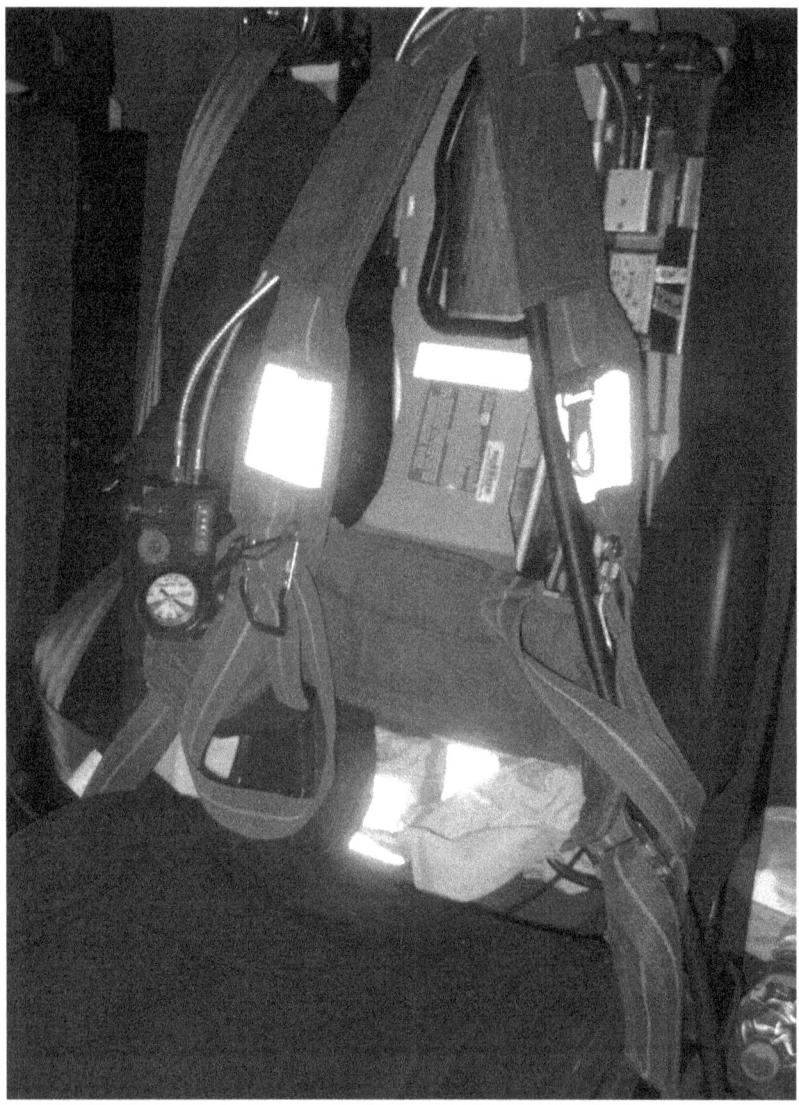

The PASS alarm.

As for the lights, there are three banks—at the entrance, in the center, and at the far end—which detect someone's presence and go on in sequence as they pass the sensors. They are all set on a timer and should then go off in sequence as well, but that's not always how they work.

"Sometimes I just walk in and only the center bank of lights is on, and no one else is here," Mike explained, perplexed. "There's no way that should happen. It's just weird."

People sitting in the Members' Room have also seen different banks of lights go on by themselves, when no one else is there. Obviously, something triggered the sensors, only it was nothing that could be seen.

"Members have told me," Robin said, "that there is *someone*, and they use that word, who walks in the main hall, between the pieces of apparatus, and one of them thinks it's his grandfather, who was a past chief here. Also, one of the kids—I call anyone younger than me a kid—was lying on the couch asleep, and something came up and slapped him upside his head! It was as if to say it's 3:00 AM and you should be home."

Mike explained that the activity is pretty much constant, but has only been so since they redid the Members' Room, which used to be three separate rooms. Did the renovations stir things up, or was it simply a case that now everyone is gathered in the same spot and they are more aware of the activity around them?

We then started talking about members of the fire department who had passed away, and Duane's EMF meter started going off. We heard about those who had died from accidents and illnesses, and of the one person who had died in the line of duty. While no one had passed away in this firehouse, which was constructed in 1985, it didn't mean that these people who had passed hadn't returned to the place that meant so much to them in life.

I asked about other activities such as voices, odors, or objects moving. Mike said that objects move all the time and they have even seen this occur on their video surveillance system. While the video hasn't actually recorded the objects being moved, it has shown things appearing in different locations, without recording anyone physically moving them.

Robin related another instance, where a member was sitting on a bench in front of the building late one night, just relaxing. Suddenly, from inside the darkened and empty firehouse, someone knocked on a window right behind him. That certainly caught his attention!

We talked about the previous firehouses in Montgomery, and while none of the old, large equipment is stored at the new firehouse, there are some small antique pieces of firefighting equipment on display here. Have some of the Old Timers come along with their equipment? As we spoke about this, both Barb and I were getting high EMF readings in the doorway that led to the Social Room, which was where the figure had been seen just the night before.

Robin and Mike look on as Barbara points to firemen
from the past she believes may still be here.

At this point, Barbara mentioned a name she had received on the way to the firehouse. She looked at the photographs of the former chiefs, and lo and behold, there was the exact name! (Even though this man passed away some time ago, I will not mention it here as he most likely still has family members in the area.) Barbara never ceases to amaze me!

As we waited for the others to arrive, I couldn't resist asking if it was okay for me to get a picture of myself on one of the fire trucks.

"And do I get to put on a hat?" I asked like a little kid, I am not ashamed to say.

Mike was kind enough to indulge my childhood desire to play fireman, and Duane took several photos of me both hanging off the back of the truck, and sitting in the driver's seat. It was one of those great perks you get being a ghost investigator, and I enjoyed every minute of it!

No matter how old you are, or what you do, who doesn't want to be a fireman for a day?

Then it was time to get serious again as the others arrived. I first interviewed Dennis, who confirmed that the banks of lights come on by themselves "all the time." And it was he who saw the figure just the night before.

"I fell asleep on the couch," Dennis began. "When I woke up, I saw something out of the corner of my eye, looked over, and there was a shadow right in front of the door. And I couldn't see the poster on the door."

"So the figure was solid?" I asked.

"Yes," Dennis replied. "Then I looked at the TV for a second and when I looked back, the shadow was gone, and I could see the poster again."

He added that the shadowy figure was about his height, but a little wider. He wasn't frightened as it all happened so fast, but he was certainly surprised—and who wouldn't be!

I then spoke to Steven, who was a witness to the PASS alarm event. He and a couple of other members were in the firehouse when, without warning, the PASS alarm went off inside the fire truck—and not gradually as they are supposed to do, but full blast all at once. When they went to investigate, the seat belt was clipped as if someone was in it! I asked him to show me where this had taken place, so I could get a better understanding and get a photograph of the equipment with the PASS alarm. As he showed me, he also explained that the air has to be flowing for the unit to work, so with everything shut off, the PASS alarm should never have activated.

Everyone is standing near the door where the figure appeared.

At this point, I went to find Barbara to see what she was picking up. I found her in the back corner and she looked a little shaken. I asked what was wrong, and she pointed to the floor where a couple of rescue dummies were sprawled out in the shadows.

"They scared the heck out of me!" Barbara replied laughing.

It reminded me of the time that Mike and I encountered a room full of mannequins in the darkness of the Columns Museum in Milford, Pennsylvania, and of the Halloween witch that was hanging from the rafters of the Burns' old farmhouse in Goshen, New York. We can now add rescue dummies to the list of things that can potentially scare the pants off of you in the middle of a ghost investigation!

I asked Barb about her overall impressions of the spirits of the firehouse, and I simply loved her eloquent and heartfelt response.

"They're here to protect them and watch over them. Whether they are alive or dead, firemen will always be family, and they'll always serve and protect each other."

I should point out that Barb has a particular affinity for the firefighting community, as her father was a fireman.

In fact, I was reminded that my father also served as a fireman for several years in Nyack, New York, after World War II. My mother told an amusing and revealing story of how just after they began dating, she watched in horror as my father stood on the roof of a burning house, seemingly oblivious to the danger. This could explain a lot about some of the genes I inherited!

I also asked Barb if there were any spirits here connected to things which might have been on the property previously. She replied that there was a man named Pete who liked to work on trucks and fancied himself a mechanic. She believed he may have lived in a house that was on or adjacent to this site. As we were talking, we passed by Dennis, and Barbara turned with the start.

"Slow it down! You have to be careful!" she said to Dennis with some urgency, taking him by surprise. "I see things like ATVs racing."

"Do you race?" I asked, and had to smile when he said he did.

Barbara warned him in the strongest terms to skip his next race, and to be much more cautious in the future. She also said that his grandfather watches over him, but that some of the things he did made his grandfather roll his eyes and shake his head. Barb went on to describe his grandfather, who had also been a firefighter, in great detail and Robin said she was describing his characteristics exactly.

Barb then turned to Mike and asked if he and this man used to bet on things.

"He would bet on anything!" Mike exclaimed, and then went on to describe how they would wager on anything and everything. In fact, where he was sitting, used to be where a poker table stood, and he described card games that would go on long into the night and get rather heated.

Barbara then turned her attention to Steven and began to describe him.

"She's got you pegged!" Mike said laughing.

Barb then spent about 45 minutes on personal readings for everyone there from spirits who were dropping by with messages for their loved ones. Barb was incredibly accurate as always, and by the end of the evening, I think the information she revealed had everyone slightly shell-shocked!

While some of the messages were quite emotional, there was one that was quite amusing. It was a former firefighter—who Barb also mentioned by name—and as his spirit was talking to Barb, he made it quite clear that he thought all of this psychic stuff was complete nonsense, although he used much stronger terms, as everyone agreed he would have done in life. You have to love the spirits who fail to see the irony in denying the possibility of communicating after death!

We all spoke for some time about the concept of firefighters being a family. This is particularly true at the Montgomery firehouse, as fathers, sons, grandsons, and wives, have served for generations here. It truly is one, big, multi-generational family, whose bonds cannot be broken, even by death.

This was one ghost investigation that was a privilege to attend. These men and women volunteer to serve and protect, and that sense of duty and obligation continues on the other side. There are most definitely spirits here, but none that should be feared. On the contrary, they are here to watch over their brother firemen, and from that we should all take comfort and be grateful for brave souls such as these.

House Call
Pine Bush, NY

I have said it before, and I will say it again, there is something strange about Pine Bush. Not only is it the "UFO Capital of the Northeast," but I believe it is also one of the most haunted locations in the region. This story came to me through Barbara Grey, of the very haunted Pine Bush House Bed and Breakfast. She arranged for us to conduct an investigation in the spring of 2015 of yet another active building in town.

It was a stormy night in June. In fact, Barbara Bleitzhofer was not sure she would be able to attend the investigation, as her town was under a tornado watch. But she braved the potentially bad weather and met my husband, Bob Strong, and I at the location. Darlene and her husband, John, arrived with the keys from the owner, Dino Mavros, to open up this vacant brick building for us. All that I knew before entering was that it had once been owned by a doctor, but had been empty for many years, and people had seen and heard some rather bizarre things there.

The air inside was stale and musty, and the décor looked untouched since the 1960s and 70s. Some windows had been vandalized, so we had to be careful of walking on broken glass, and a ceiling in one room had partially collapsed. Other than that, the building appeared to be strong and well built, with beautiful wood floors, moulding, and stained glass. Thanks to information I later obtained from realtor RJ Smith, I found out that the house was built around 1910.

RJ Smith Realty occupies the house next door, and Mr. Smith was able to furnish me with the following post card in which his house is on the right, and the brick building is the structure in the middle. The doctor who bought that building in the 1950s, Dr. Ciliberto, was actually Mr. Smith's doctor when he was growing up. Although he was not sure when the doctor changed the structure, it's plain to see it underwent major renovations. The porch was removed, the exterior was covered in bricks, and a wing was also added in the back, just off the kitchen.

The house (in the middle) as it looked c. 1910.   Courtesy of RJ Smith.

Mr. Smith informed me that Dr. Ciliberto was a "typical country doctor," who retired in the mid 1970s and moved to Florida. Since then, there were only two occupants for very brief periods of time—the doctor's son, who lived on the top floor for about a year, and another doctor who rented the newer wing for about a year.

Other than that, during the last 40 years the only time the house has been used is for the very popular and creative Halloween night haunted house event hosted by Smith Realty, Dino Mavros, and the Town of Wallkill Boys & Girls Clubs. Each year there is a theme, and past themes have included the "Dead Rock Café" with volunteers dressing like deceased rock stars (they even had an airplane on the lawn for Buddy Holly!), and a crashed UFO theme with aliens abducting and experimenting on humans. While it's a wonderful event and all in good fun, this house probably doesn't need volunteers to act like ghosts—the ghosts here do well enough on their own, as we were about to find out!

When we first entered, I was surprised by the size of the interior and the number of rooms stretching back in the addition and up the three expansive floors. I was also quite surprised—and even somewhat startled—by the intensity of the atmosphere in the place. Much to my dismay, it reminded me of the frenetic, chaotic, and disturbing energies of the asylums and mental hospitals I have investigated. I don't know what I was expecting, but I can assure you I was not expecting this.

As we began our walkthrough, John told me that one day when he was on the third floor, he heard a voice clearly whisper, "Hey!" No one else was around at a time, and he is absolutely certain of what he heard. We were all to hear whispering and voices during the course of the night, so I have no doubt that this is a relatively common occurrence here, if I can use that term under these circumstances.

Before getting started, Barbara said that on the trip there, she had told her husband that she had the sense that this had to "be a medical place in the old days." Sure enough, her immediate reaction upon entering was that there was a spirit named Bruce, who had come to this place for treatment for a broken arm. Bruce was to make his presence known several times during the evening and Barb did not hesitate to classify him as "not a nice person."

Perhaps it was even Bruce who was responsible for something that occurred within minutes of us starting the initial walkthrough to get oriented. I was standing in a front parlor near an old, console television, and Barbara was to my right. I was holding up my digital recorder in my right hand and all of a sudden my right shoulder began pivoting forward. I didn't feel a hand or any type of force or object pushing on me, just the involuntary movement of the right side of my body twisting forward.

At the same moment, I was looking at Barb and she suddenly lurched forward as if she had been roughly shoved from behind.

"We're being pushed!" she announced.

Obviously, someone did not appreciate the fact that we were there, but I certainly didn't appreciate being pushed, either! It was definitely "game on," and I wasn't leaving until I got what I came for—evidence that this place was very haunted.

Barbara and I were both pushed in this room.

Just after that incident, John told us that the upstairs was "way creepier." I replied that we liked "way creepier," but I was half hoping that didn't mean anymore physical contact with angry spirits.

We went next to the rooms off of the kitchen that stretched beyond the back of the main house. The first room had clearly been an exam room and it made my skin crawl. Barb heard some whispering, but couldn't tell from where it was originating. We went all the way back to the last room where we came upon a lot of the Halloween decorations being stored.

Thank heaven we did not enter the room in total darkness, as there was a life-sized mannequin which probably would have scared the heck out of us. As things were already very tense, we took a few moments to catch our breath and pose with the mannequin. Then Barb asked me to take a picture of her in the coffin prop.

"It's the one and only time I'll know I'm in one," she stated.

"Oh, *you'll* know," I didn't hesitate to respond, knowing full well that something simple like death couldn't stop her unique abilities.

Barbara and I with our new friend.
(I think I dated this guy in college…)

Once our brief amusement was over, I declared it was time to get serious, and it got serious very quickly. We went up to the second floor where we encountered the unhappy spirit of an old, sick woman who had trouble breathing. Barb and I both felt like crying, as this woman's spirit was so heavy and depressing. Barb believed her name had been Isabel, and she had struggled in great discomfort in her final days here. Whether Isabel had stayed here during the time the doctor owned the building, or she had lived in the house in its early days, we couldn't determine for sure, but regardless, the feeling was quite disturbing.

About this time, John heard what he described as a "swoosh" sound, and Darlene was to hear that same sound downstairs later on. I commented that I was "constantly on edge" in this place, moments before Barb said that she heard a voice telling us to "get out." The activity was really ratcheting up quickly!

In the rear of the second floor was a room with two hospital beds in it, making us think that this was more than simply a place for people to stop by and get a checkup. However, RJ Smith said, to his knowledge, there was never any long term care here with Dr. Ciliberto.

"This was more than just a house. *Way* more," Barb whispered to me. "People were here because no one wanted them anymore."

She felt that there may have been people with dementia and other serious physical and mental issues. If so, perhaps they predated Dr. Ciliberto, and stayed here sometime between 1910 and the 1950s. She also felt that at one point, a patient had stabbed someone with a knitting needle. It did indeed have the feel of a mental institution, and I once again commented that I couldn't remember the last time I was so on edge in a location.

Meanwhile, Bob scanned the entire structure with the EMF meter, but he didn't get any unusual readings. However, whether it was from the

One of the hospital beds with a Bible with a bookmark in Judges 11.

impending storms, or something paranormal, there was palpable electricity in the air, and both Barbara and John saw what they described as white balls or orbs moving about in several rooms.

We then made our way into an expansive rec room on the second floor, which contained a pool table, record player, and an old refrigerator. I found a box of color slides, some of which had pictures of Pine Bush in the 1950s or 60s. Darlene came upon a stack of old appointment books from 1967 to 1975. While there were no detailed patient records, there were the names of patients with a brief description of why they were making the appointment. While such records may hold valuable information about the place, I did realize that some of these people may still be alive and still living in the area, so I decided not to reveal any of the private information these books contained.

There was a bathroom on this floor in the rear of the building, and Barbara saw someone moving inside. When we entered, she got the sense that there had been a lot of babies in that room. Had women also come here to give birth?

"This room gives me pressure," she stated.

"This whole house gives me pressure!" I responded, trying to deal with the overload of sensations that made it difficult to focus and concentrate.

In yet another bedroom on the second floor, Barbara encountered a man in jeans and a dark shirt standing near the closet. She got the sense that he may have been handicapped and was either a drug user or was being heavily medicated.

"He doesn't want to be alone, but now he is," she explained about the sad figure. "He is not happy here."

In the front room of the second floor, John asked what we felt when we entered. We all responded that on this hot and oppressively humid day, this room somehow felt cool. John was using one of those ghost hunting apps on his cell phone, and he turned it around to show us that it had generated the word "cool" when he had entered that room! It was either a remarkable coincidence, or something was trying to communicate with us through his phone.

One of the many odd things I noticed about this house was that the rooms had many closets, and in those closets there were as many as three sets of electrical outlets. Why would anyone need so many outlets in a closet? There were also sinks and bathrooms in several of the rooms, as well as a number of kitchens. Were these used as apartments at some point, or were they for some type of long term medical care? There were also old intercom panels installed in many of the rooms, which lent strength to the idea that this had been more than just a residence and medical office at some point.

Navigating broken glass on the staircase to the attic/third floor, we found it had been finished with wood paneling, and had several small, low storerooms on the sides. Here again, we found an intercom and a fully equipped kitchen.

"We are being followed, and I don't feel safe," Barbara blurted out in an uncharacteristic admission, summing up what she had been feeling from the minute we entered this house. "This is one of those places that *freaks* me out!"

In fact, this feeling became so overwhelming that at one point, she had to physically put her back against the wall to try to prevent the many spirits from coming up behind and around her. As we were descending the staircase back to the second floor, though, she said that despite how

One of the storerooms in the attic apartment.

intense the many spirits were, they were "not vicious."

I wasn't sure if I completely agreed with her, as I felt somewhat threatened on that staircase, as if someone there wouldn't mind inflicting some harm on the living, possibly by shoving them down the stairs. At that very moment, John said his ghost hunting app indicated the words "thrown," and "attack."

"Great!" I said sarcastically, carefully watching my every step.

Under the staircase there was a short door and cramped, little closet. The door was stuck, but I asked Bob to open it as I had the strongest feeling that someone had once been closed up in there, and had tried desperately to beat their way out. Sure enough, there was no latch or handle on the inside, and there were deep gouges as if someone had repeatedly struck the inside of the door, trying to hammer their way out with a heavy object.

Back on the first floor, I asked for a sign if any spirits were present. I then specifically asked if there were any spirits of children, and from somewhere in the house there was one deep, resounding banging sound. I waited a little while and asked again, and we all heard two deep, banging noises, followed by the sounds of someone walking on the second floor above us. As remarkable as the banging sounds were, the footsteps were even more amazing, as the second floor is heavily carpeted, and it isn't physically possible to be able to generate the sound of shoes on hardwood floors—at least not for those of us that are alive.

When we returned to the first exam room off of the kitchen, I asked if there were any former patients there. There was no response. I then asked if someone had died here, and I swear I heard a scratchy type of voice whisper, "Yes." Darlene also heard the sound, which she described as "high-pitched," but she could not determine what it was saying.

Continuing with that line of questioning, I asked who had died here, and told them to come and talk to us. On cue, I heard male voices coming from the doorways on both sides of the room, from my right and from my left. John was in the hall beyond the doorway to my right and he reported hearing "many whispering voices" around him. Barbara specifically heard the voices coming from our left. It's difficult to describe such a moment—a moment when you feel that you are surrounded by many disembodied souls. I have no doubt that we would all swear in court to hearing those whispering voices around us in that exam room!

In my head, I also kept hearing the number 23, so I wondered out loud what it could possibly mean. After thinking for a short time I asked if 23 people had died in this building. Darlene was recording everything that was being said, and she reported that both times I said the number 23, there was a 23 being displayed as part of her audio counter. Barbara also felt that 23 deaths was an accurate accounting of what had gone on here in the one hundred years of it being both a residence (people often died at home in the early 20th century) and a doctor's office. Whether or not we can find documentation to back that up, that number of deaths would certainly go a long way to explain all of the activity in the house—especially considering just one restless spirit is enough to wreak havoc.

Back in the television room where Barb and I had previously been pushed, several of us saw some sort of light moving around the room. John heard a little girl's voice, from a child of perhaps four or five years old. She had said one or two words, although he couldn't make out what they were.

"This has to be one of the creepiest places we've ever been!" Barbara exclaimed, which is saying a lot, considering all the places we have investigated over the years. "There is a *lot* of activity."

"Yes," I agreed. "A lot, and for a lot of different reasons."

"Honestly," Barbara continued, "I wouldn't want to be here alone after dark. And no one could be comfortable living here."

I can't stress enough how intense every moment was in this bizarre building. It was physically and emotionally draining, but I still wanted to remain in order to get some footage on the camcorder. Bob went back to the second floor with me as I set up the camcorder, aiming it down the hallway towards the rec room. Looking through the viewfinder, I saw that it was still light enough that I could switch it off from the infrared setting to natural light. I did so, and then double-checked that I still had a good image. Once I was sure it was recording properly, Bob and I revisited the other rooms on the second floor to see if there was any additional activity.

After about 10 minutes or so, we came back down the hall so that I could retrieve the camcorder. I looked through the viewfinder to make sure the image was still good, and was disappointed to see that the camera had shut itself off and was no longer recording. I assumed the battery must have gone dead, although it was fully charged with over 400 minutes of time. But that was not the problem. I found that the switch on the side of the camcorder *had physically been moved to the off position!* It is simply not possible for this camcorder to move that switch on its own. Someone or something had to *physically flip that switch* to turn it off.

Something turned off the switch on this camcorder.

I switched it back on just to make sure it was all right, and it resumed recording normally. It wasn't until I got home and was able to review the footage that I found that the camcorder had indeed recorded for those ten minutes, and only switched off *just as Bob and I were approaching it.* You can clearly hear us coming down the hall and we had to have been within just a couple of feet away when that switch was flipped.

As the switch makes a distinctive clicking sound, we should have heard it. We also should have seen someone—if there was anyone visible—standing by the camcorder, but there was no one there. This literally happened right in front of us, right under the noses of the ghost investigators, but we saw and heard nothing.

"I think we got what we came for," I said to Bob, as I marveled at this in-your-face paranormal event.

We came downstairs and I was all excited to share the news, but Barbara, Darlene, and John were not in the parlor or kitchen. We called out to them and searched the back rooms, but they were nowhere to be found.

"What the hell?" I asked, as we wondered where they could possibly be. Given the timing, their apparent disappearance was a little too unnerving, but then we heard Barbara's voice outside.

They had been searching the exterior of the building, looking for any signs of the age of the place, hoping that there might be a date in a cornerstone or plaque, but found nothing. I told them about the exciting camcorder incident, and my story was punctuated by an ominous clap of thunder.

The sky was darkening rapidly, and the wind was picking up, so we decided it was time to get out of Dodge and try to get home safely in the event there was severe weather about to strike. Fortunately, we were all spared, but I later read in the newspaper that a nearby town had been hit with over 100 mph winds that left a path of destruction over 2 miles wide! That would have been excitement that none of us needed, particularly that night.

So what do I think about this former Victorian house, turned brick doctor's office, turned Halloween haunted house? In short, it is one of the most intense places we have investigated. There is a lot going on here, and I think there is a lot more to discover.

What dark secrets may be hiding in its shadows? If the Ghost Investigator ever makes another house call to this doctor's home, perhaps those secrets will be revealed.

This sign at the front entrance (used for the haunted house event) says it all!

Desmond House Revisited
Mount Saint Mary's College, Newburgh, NY

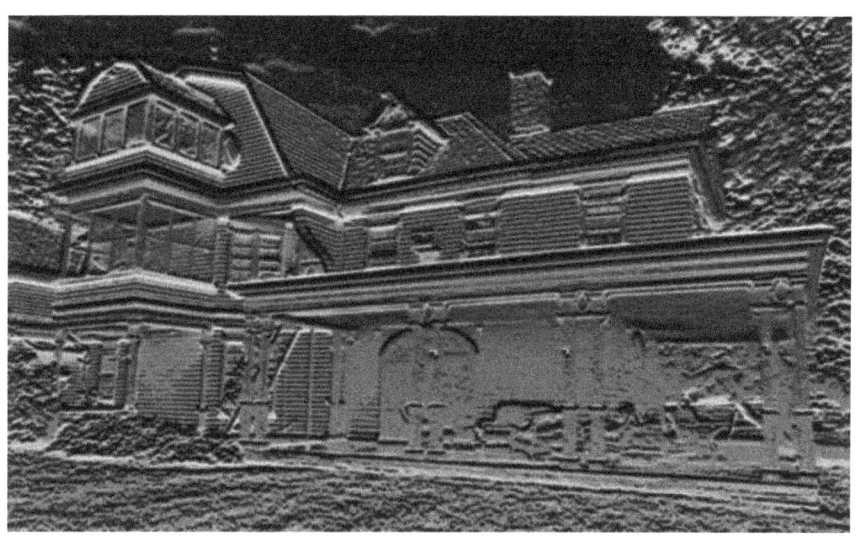

I first wrote about the Desmond House in Volume 12 of my *Ghost Investigator* series. I had given lectures there several times–which is how I knew the place was haunted—but I had been unable to be there when psychic Barbara Bleitzhofer and Duane Smith went to investigate. However, in September of 2014, staff members Sandy Brandman and Jackie Gerace were kind enough to allow us to come back.

Michael Worden and I naturally stopped for our ritual Chinese buffet before meeting Barb and Duane in the parking lot of the Desmond House, which is part of Mount Saint Mary's College. Our first indication that it might be an interesting night was when Mike was trying to set up his Trifield EMF meter and the alarm refused to turn off.

Normal procedure is to set the meter down and then adjust the sensitivity until the alarm goes quiet. Then if a person–or a spirit–comes close to the meter, the alarm should gently sound. However, for some reason, the meter was acting in the exact opposite way that it should have. The alarm would not shut off *until* Mike got close to it, which makes absolutely no sense!

We all sat down at the large dining room table and Sandy recalled that the first time Barbara was there, she mentioned that a former cook with an accent was still there; a woman they had simply called Cook. Just as Barbara was saying that she remembered encountering Cook, there was a loud noise in the next room. I asked what room that was, and Sandy replied that it was the kitchen, which made sense if the cook was there with us.

"Cook, do you have a message for us?" I asked.

A moment later we all heard voices, which were hard to pinpoint, but seemed to be coming from somewhere outside, although we couldn't see anyone out on the lawn.

As the former owner of the house, Thomas Desmond, had been a successful businessman and politician, he was definitely someone who was used to being in charge. Barbara had mentioned that Thomas was not exactly thrilled about having people poking around in *his* house, so Mike decided to see if he could prompt a reaction.

"I know you don't like other men in your house," Mike began, "but I'm here now and I'm not leaving."

BANG!

The sudden noise in the adjacent room startled us and was clearly audible on my digital recorder. We all heard it, and could not find any explanation for it–other than that perhaps Thomas was not happy about Mike's presence.

But it got even stranger.

"I'm the man of the house tonight," Mike declared.

Our blood ran cold when there was a low, moaning sound behind me and Barb. I can't impress upon you enough how creepy it sounded, and it truly made my skin crawl.

Just a moment later, something very odd happened in the room right behind Mike, where Barbara had set up her green laser grid, which shines a pattern of sharp points of light across an entire room so you can detect any kind of movement. As Mike continued to declare his Alpha Male status, a diffuse green light suddenly appeared above the fireplace mantel on the grid field. At first it moved with a jump, and then it steadily slid over and downward until it disappeared at floor level.

We were all floored by the remarkable sight and everyone was covered in goose bumps. The diffuse green light then appeared in the middle of the room again for a few moments, but then it was gone for good. Barbara checked her laser light, which was mounted on a tripod, and found that it was secure and couldn't possibly have moved on its own. But even if the mount or the tripod had slipped, the entire grid of points of light should have shifted together, not just a single point. It is simply impossible for only one light to go "rogue" in that manner.

The laser light grid in which the diffuse green light appeared and moved.

Excitement and tension were now definitely at a fever pitch, and before Mike could continue his challenges to Thomas Desmond, I heard a loud sound outside of the house and ran to a window to see what was happening. There was a car out in front of the building and a man was standing next to his open trunk. This was very suspicious, as Sandy had told the security guards to stay away and not to disturb us until we were finished. There were no classes scheduled, and the house was completely dark. So what was this man doing here at this hour?

Sandy went to the front door to find out, but when she turned the key it snapped in the lock! How much force does it take to snap a key? There's no way that by her simply trying to unlock the door, which they did every day, this key should suddenly break and make it impossible to open the door. Sandy and Jackie then decided to go out the kitchen door and see what this man wanted. As the circumstances seemed very suspicious, I asked Mike to go out with them in case this guy was up to no good.

So, what was this mysterious young man doing outside the Desmond House in the dark, with his trunk open? He was trying to deliver a pizza! The order had come in from the Guzman building back at the main campus two miles away, and the delivery man mistakenly came to the Desmond House. In all the years Sandy and Jackie have been there, no one has ever gotten a pizza delivery, nor had anyone ever tried to deliver one by mistake. Yet here, in the midst of all this paranormal craziness with the banging sounds, voices, strange groan, moving green light, and the key snapping off in the front door, this was the moment for the errant pizza delivery!

Duane's photo of us all in the central room where the green light appeared and many of the noises originated. From left to right: Jackie, Mike, me, Sandy and Barbara.

We all had a good laugh over it and reconvened back at the dining room table, and attempted to get the investigation back on track, but as soon as we sat down, the green laser grid went completely dark. Barb, Mike, and I had each brought extra sets of AAA batteries with us for just such an event, but they all appeared to be dead, even though they had never been used before! We were just about to give up on the laser grid, when it came back on by itself and was fine the rest of the night.

Mike's infrared photo of Barbara in intense concentration in the dining room.

Jackie then related to us that the window shades in her office always move themselves. She likes them at a specific height, but she will return to her office and they will be in a different position. They suspect that Thomas likes things to be the way he always kept them. Jackie also said she heard her name being whispered right by her ear one day. I guess you can get used to anything, but these are very strange circumstances under which to work!

A short time later, I heard footsteps coming up behind me and quickly looked around the room to see that everyone was there but Duane.

"That better be you Duane, walking in," I said, "or I'm running!"

Fortunately, it was indeed Duane, who had just been in the other room to take some photographs.

Our attention so far had been focused on the man of the house, Thomas Desmond, but we now turned to his lovely and talented wife, Alice. As soon as Barbara asked for a sign from Alice, the laser grid doubled in brightness! There was also a deep rumbling sound, which we at first attributed to an approaching thunderstorm, but a short time later I checked the sky and found it was clear, and there were no storms in the area.

We then asked for another sign from Alice, and the small elevator she used when she had become crippled from arthritis suddenly turned itself on.

"I don't believe this!" I exclaimed. "The freakin' elevator just went off!"

In a heartbeat, I was out of my chair and running toward the elevator. I stood there for several minutes with my meters and cameras, breathlessly waiting for something else to happen, but nothing did. The next day, Sandy spoke to the caretaker, who said that the elevator automatically 'adjusts itself' on occasion. That is certainly good to know, however, the timing of the events, just as we were asking for a sign from Alice, still puts this in the category of *remarkable* in my book. And there would be an even more startling elevator incident later on that evening.

We then headed upstairs, and as we all stood in Mrs. Desmond's former bedroom, Jackie and Barb heard a swishing sound out in the hall, as if something was moving or flapping around.

Mike made the comment that he was in Mrs. Desmond's bedroom, but declared he was going to go into Mr. Desmond's private room, and with those words the green laser grid that Barb had set up upstairs flickered several times and we all "oohed and aahed" at the display. And when Mike stepped into Mr. Desmond's room, a rush of cold air went through him. Mike had definitely made himself *persona non grata* in the Desmond household!

I tried to take a picture of Mike in that room, but my camera flash simply refused to work. Duane told me the same thing had been happening repeatedly to his camera throughout the house, and he remarked that we were all going to have a lot of dark pictures.

On the third floor in Alice's studio, I kept feeling as if there was something (or someone) behind me. I turned around several times to look, but didn't see anything, so I asked Barb if she was able to sense anything near me. She said there was a red rectangle of energy above me, and it had a yellow border around it.

"What does *that* mean?" I asked, having no clue why there would be a red box with a yellow border.

"Red is the color of anger," Barb explained, "and yellow is friendliness."

I thought for a moment, but was still puzzled.

"So let me get this straight," I said laughing, "it's anger framed in friendship!?"

However, I wasn't laughing for long, as the strange feeling grew into one of fear, as if someone used to hide here to feel safe. I asked Mike to stand in the same spot and let me know if he felt anything. After just a few moments, he expressed the same sentiments that someone who was afraid used to come to this room to hide for some reason. Did Alice have anything to fear from either of her husbands? Or, was this a frightened spirit from other residents of this house, the house which stood on the spot previously, or from an even earlier time? It's impossible to know for sure, but when two people experience the same exact feelings and impressions on the same spot, it is definitely worth noting.

After going through all the other rooms and offices in this expansive building, we once again went back to the dining room. On the digital recorder you can hear my voice saying that this had been the hub of activity that evening, and then Mike said, "Mr. Desmond, I'm back."

Just then, there was the most bizarre squealing type noise, which was loud enough to clearly be recorded. We all heard it, and we all assumed it was someone's gurgling stomach, but we went person by person around the room to ascertain whose digestive system was making the unearthly noises, and one by one, we each said, "No, it wasn't me." If so, then it was one of the most chilling sounds I ever heard or recorded, and it could best be described as a Hollywood special effects sound of a ghostly "*woooooo*."

"I thought for sure, Mike, it was the Chinese buffet coming back to haunt you," I said.

"It definitely wasn't me!" he responded adamantly.

We discussed the eerie sound for a few minutes and found that each of us had heard it originating from a different place. For example, I thought it came from across the room, while Barb and Duane thought it came from somewhere behind me. As we spoke about the strange sound, there was another one of those thunder-like rumblings again, followed by the distinct sound of men's voices. Once again, we could not pinpoint the origin of these voices, and as we compared notes we found that they seemed to be all around us.

As if things weren't intense enough, Jackie mentioned the basement and said that we could go down there, but it was "creepy as hell."

"We are *so* into that!" Duane said, not hesitating for a moment to volunteer to go into the basement.

"You had me at *creepy*," I added, standing up and grabbing my equipment.

The basement was enormous, but it didn't have a particularly scary appearance. One strange thing, though, was bright red door with a sign reading "Furniture Room," which had a small window with sturdy metal bars. Why would anyone need a prison–like door on a storage room in the basement? Had it been part of the earlier structure? Did it once have a more nefarious purpose?

One basement in which I wouldn't want to be locked!
Photo courtesy of Michael Worden.

As we wandered around the dark basement, Duane saw a bright flash of light in an adjoining room and thought that one of us had just taken a picture. However, when he went into that room, he found that nobody was in there, and it did not connect to any other rooms.

The one truly creepy thing down there, were the large cobwebs that would brush against your arm and get in your hair if you weren't careful. I joked with Mike that there were probably Peruvian Death Spiders in those webs (a running joke since encountering the spider in the embalming sinks at the Patchett House I wrote about in *Ghost Investigator Volume 9*), and he responded that at the very least, there were most likely clowns hiding in the shadows (the only thing he hates more than spiders).We were clearly getting punchy after the very intense and active night's investigation!

The paranormal fun and games were not yet over, however. Back in the dining room again, Barb asked for Alice to knock on something or give us a sign. Immediately, the elevator loudly clicked on again, and both Barbara and I actually jumped in our seats.

"Alice, are you going to bed or are you going to join us?" Sandy asked.

A moment later, Sandy, Duane, and I heard footsteps on the second floor above us. They were soft footsteps, which could have come from someone of the stature of the elderly Alice Desmond, and they also seemed to be going down the hallway to her former bedroom. I hurried over to the elevator and listened, and it definitely sounded like someone was moving around on the second floor. We all waited quietly for a while, but nothing else happened.

"It's as if the whole feeling in the house has shifted," Mike said, referring to the peace and calm which appeared to have finally descended over the house.

"It's like everyone went to bed," Barb said, agreeing that everything now felt calm.

Not everything had settled down completely, though, as Barbara tried to get one last response by asking if someone would knock back when she tapped on the table. There was no knocking in reply, but we heard that same bizarre squealing again! And once again, each of us denied that our digestive system was the culprit.

In conclusion, it was an exciting, eventful, and draining investigation– just the way we like them! I truly believe that Thomas and Alice Desmond still occupy the home they loved so much. And they are not alone, either, as there are several other spirits in the house and on the grounds. While Mr. Desmond may not be the friendliest of ghostly hosts, he is never threatening, nor is anything else that we have ever encountered here.

I urge you to go to one of the special events held at the Desmond House, or attend one of their lectures or classes. And while you are there, keep your sixth sense on high alert. Most of all, please be polite to the former residents. If not, be prepared to experience a chilling cold, an unearthly sound, or perhaps even a mysterious pizza delivery!

Mike took this infrared image of me at the dining room table as strange noises are all around us in the dark.

North Church Street
Goshen, NY

When I first moved to Orange County, NY in the 1990s, there was a marvelous bakery in Goshen, in a beautiful old house on North Church Street. I would get up early on many Sunday mornings to pick up fresh rolls and pastries for breakfast.

One day, when I was giving a ghost lecture at the Goshen Library, someone told me that the bakery building was haunted. In the following years, many people said the same thing, but the bakery went out of business and I never got to speak to any of the employees. Imagine my surprise, then, when I was at the eye doctor in Monroe and the woman who was helping me with my glasses mentioned that she used to live upstairs in that house, and the place was very haunted!

The following is a synopsis of what she told me:

- I moved into the apartment on North Church Street in the mid-80s, and we lived there for about five years. When we first moved in, the place had a little strangeness about it, but nothing really crazy happened. My little cousin at the time was about two, and she would not go into the bathroom area, and she would always cry. In the house at the time, there was a florist on the bottom floor and an apartment behind it, and we had the apartment upstairs. The front of the house upstairs was closed off, for what reason I don't know. I also don't know how long it was before some of the strange things started to happen.
- I am a sensitive, so I think I felt things before it got really crazy. The first thing was that my mom was tapped on her shoulder when no one was in the house. One night I was lying in bed and something scratched me across my shoulder. I don't know what it was. I was a little freaked out by it, to say the least.
- A lot of the really bad things started when they were working on the house and I did the stupid thing with playing with the Ouija board. I did not have a door on my bedroom. I collected dolls, and I had two dolls in this bell thing hanging in the doorway, and they would start to move by themselves.

- We had to move because a bakery was moving in downstairs and they were going to move the lady that lived in the apartment downstairs up to our apartment. So when we were getting ready to move, the house felt like chaos. I was afraid to sleep in my room. I would sleep on the floor of my mom's room with my bible in my hands. I was 17, I was not a little kid. I never slept in her room before or after we left there.
- When we were packing, I opened my closet door to get some stuff we had stored on the side of it. (The roof leaked so I only put stuff to one side of it.) When we opened it, there was writing on the wall that said, "John was here." John was the man that lived downstairs, who passed away maybe six months to a year earlier.
- After we moved out, we saw the lady that now lived in our apartment. She told us that one night she was lying in bed and something pushed down on her bed, and she then felt like something was choking her. She was very much frightened. She had lived in that house for years. She moved out not too long after they moved her upstairs.
- I spoke to the person who, years later, opened the photo studio in the house. He said that he did not pay much attention to the photos that were not perfect, because he took so many of them and they were digital. He did say that no matter what, his feet were always cold there. I also had a mailman tell me he has heard stories of that house being haunted.

This house obviously has stories to tell! What tragedy occurred here, and why does the spirit or spirits appear to want to harm the living? If anyone knows the history of this place, or has any additional information on this house, please contact me.

Museum Village
Monroe, New York

When staff and visitors see the little girl with the blond pigtails, wearing an old-fashioned pinafore dress, walking through Museum Village in Monroe, New York, they think she is a very realistic addition to the re-creation of this 19th century town. There's only one slight problem; she is not a real flesh and blood child. But she is a very real ghost!

This little girl, whom everyone calls Claire, is just one of the many spirits attached to this wonderful living history museum, founded in 1950 by Roscoe Smith. Smith was the wealthy founder of Orange and Rockland Utilities, and an avid collector of antiques. Over the years, he amassed an astounding 27,000 artifacts, but that statement requires some clarification. For example, he didn't only collect one inkwell; he may have collected ten or twenty of them. However, when the staff conducted an inventory several years ago, all of those inkwells were considered one item. So, that number of 27,000 is somewhat deceiving, as the total number of pieces in the collection is actually many times more.

Founder Roscoe Smith, who many people believe
still walks around Museum Village.

The best way for any collector to admire his artifacts is to display them, and have the ability to show them to others so that they may also appreciate the history or beauty of the items. Most of us are happy to have a display case or cabinet to show off whatever we have collected, but when you own a major utility company, and have acres of land from your old family farm, you can build an entire village to share your collection with the world.

In 1950, Museum Village opened its doors, and if you were a child going to any of the schools in the area since then, chances are you took a class trip here, and then took your own kids, and maybe grandkids decades later. What you may not have realized on your visits, is that only one structure—the log cabin, circa 1780–is original, and the other buildings were new construction designed to accurately recreate original structures. However, when you step inside any of the more than two dozen buildings open to the public, and see that everything in the interior is a geuine antique, dating from the period being portrayed, you have no problem feeling like you have just stepped back in time.

Memorial to Roscoe Smith. Note the chickens roaming free.

For example, the drugstore is as authentic as you can get, as Smith purchased the entire contents of a pharmacy in the town of Florida, New York, including every medicine bottle, display case, countertop, right down to the fabulous marble soda fountain where ladies in long dresses and boys in knickers used to enjoy a refreshing beverage before getting back on their horses and carriages.

As spirits can attach themselves to people, places, and things, it is simple math to deduce that there are at least 27,000 possibilities of hauntings here at Museum Village. And let's not forget the many ghosts who are wandering the property. All in all, it would not surprise me if there were at least a few dozen spirits here.

It was a warm, sunny day in June of 2015, when I sat down with the Executive Director, Michael Sossler, and the Program Director, Lori

Siccardi, to talk about what staff and visitors have experienced over the years.

Interior of the authentic drugstore.

While Michael has not personally experienced anything during the five years he has worked here—and he has been on the property at all hours of the day and night—enough people have shared their experiences that he may have to soften his skepticism to account for all the credible eyewitness sightings.

Lori, on the other hand, is something of "a ghost magnet." In her fifteen years working at Museum Village, she has had more experiences than I could probably list in this book. However, when I asked her what was the first thing she noticed that wasn't normal, she replied that to her way of thinking, all of this activity *is* normal—an attitude I wish more people would adopt as it would make my job a lot easier!

Perhaps the most common sighting is that of Claire, the little girl who appears to be somewhere between seven to twelve years old. She has been seen by Lori, a security guard, and a number of people who had no prior knowledge of this blond, pigtailed ghost. She has most often been seen near the schoolhouse, but is not restricted to that building.

The one-room schoolhouse.

In fact, one employee who saw Claire, felt her presence with him in his car as he was driving home, which must have been incredibly unnerving! Fortunately, he felt her presence in the car again the next day on his drive to work, and felt as though she came back to Museum Village, and didn't remain to haunt him at his house.

The quaint, one-room schoolhouse, which is an accurate re-creation of an early 1800s school in Monroe, New York, where Smith's grandmother taught classes, also has the spirit of a young boy, and some people have said they have heard the sounds of many children talking and laughing inside, only to find the building empty. Have all these spirits become attached to the schoolhouse artifacts, or did they come to this property with the rest of the collection of children's clothing, toys, and furniture, and they now all congregate in this room to be together with other children?

The interior of the schoolhouse.

The other spirit that is seen most often is that of the founder himself, Roscoe Smith. Many people over the years have seen him walking the property or standing inside the buildings. Lori told me that on a recent ghost hunt–which they host here at least once a month–a woman had a K2 EMF meter, and every time they mentioned Roscoe's name, the meter lit up!

As Lori, Michael, and I sat at a big table in the main building at the entrance to Museum Village, discussing Roscoe Smith, I heard someone walking around in the adjacent room. There were also some banging noises, as if someone was doing some work or moving heavy items. As neither Lori nor Michael paid any attention to these sounds, I just assumed another member of the staff was going about their business, whatever that could have been. However, a few minutes later, all the sounds stopped and I never saw anyone exit that room, so I asked who was in there. I was quite surprised to find out that no one else was in the building with us!

"I would have said something sooner about all the sounds," I explained, "but neither of you took any notice, so I didn't think it was anything unusual."

Lori and Michael explained that they are so used to strange sounds that they really don't pay much attention to them anymore. I guess that's what comes from working all day in an incredibly haunted location—the paranormal is truly normal here!

Now that I was on full alert, a short time later I paused to report that I thought I saw someone passing by one of the windows. I watched for a few more moments but didn't see anything else. However, a minute later someone did come inside—a real, living, breathing person, so that is who I must have seen.

Lori had another fascinating Roscoe Smith story to share. Because nothing is normal here, the sanitation man also happens to be a psychic medium, who often claims to see Smith when he stops by to collect payment for his services. One day, Lori had asked him if he could see Smith that day.

"Yes, I see him, but he is doing something so silly I don't even want to tell you," the man said, uncharacteristically shy about his connection with the other world.

It took some coaxing, but finally the man revealed what he saw—the spirit of Roscoe Smith was wearing a pointy, party hat, and extending a bouquet of flowers toward Lori. Rather than laugh at the image, Lori was stunned. Just that morning—long before the sanitation man arrived—Lori had been discussing with Michael that Roscoe Smith's 135th birthday was coming up. To celebrate the milestone, she wanted to have a birthday party with cupcakes and *party hats*! Apparently, Smith heard this conversation and greatly appreciated what Lori wanted to do.

Lori then told the story of one of the maintenance men (who was not born in the United States) who came to her first thing one morning, all excited. "I saw someone! I saw a man in a uniform!" he said in his heavy accent. The soldier was walking across the property and looked so real that this employee ran after him, thinking he was an intruder. But even though this man in uniform was just walking and the maintenance man was running, he could not "close the gap" between them and was unable to catch up with him.

Perhaps the fact that this soldier then disappeared into thin air was the reason why he could not be apprehended! As this man was not from this country, and therefore not familiar with the variety of our military uniforms, he was unfortunately unable to say from which era this soldier had stepped to walk the property.

Several paranormal investigation teams have come to Museum Village over the years, and one group in particular was not well received by the spirits. The livery stable houses a unique collection of carriages and sleighs, and among them are not one, not two, but three hearses! There is also an old horse-drawn ambulance, which, given the state of medicine way back when, might as well have also doubled as a hearse. And given the paranormal potential of these objects, it probably wasn't the wisest course of action when this group of investigators went out of their way to try to antagonize the spirits in the stable. Their efforts were rewarded by a threatening voice telling them to get out!

One of the hearses.

One of the most popular events at Museum Village is their Pure Terror Screampark, held every Halloween season. This scary attraction draws many visitors every year, and some of them get more than they bargained for, in the form of actual ghost sightings. But given the nature of several of the haunted houses and the haunted trail, we can only wonder how many other people do not report their sightings because they think it is simply great special effects?

After discussing all of these fascinating ghost stories, I couldn't wait to see the actual locations of the sightings. It was immediately evident why 19th century spirits would feel comfortable here, as you feel like you have truly entered another time and place. Our first stop was the schoolhouse, and my initial impression was that we were not alone inside this building. There was certainly nothing threatening about these spirits, so I could easily believe that they are just playful children looking to reconnect with the world they left at such early ages.

The livery stable was an entirely different ball of paranormal wax. It was almost an effort to walk into the building, with its very heavy atmosphere. Having been a ghost investigator for almost two decades now, I can usually tell when a building contains contented or disturbed spirits. Whoever inhabits the livery stable at Museum Village is not a happy camper, and I think he has a lot of unhappy and disturbed company with him. It was certainly nice to step back out into the sunshine and fresh air.

The general store was a marvel. I could just imagine the thrill experienced by the men, women, and children, living on isolated farms, as they entered this store to see the huge variety of tools, fabrics, toys, and everyday necessities for sale. And how many hours, days, and years did the local men gather around the big pot-bellied stove, discussing the business—and gossip—of their communities and the country? It is worth bringing your children to Museum Village just for this country store alone, to show them that life did not always revolve around the mega shopping malls of today.

The drugstore is another perfect time capsule. As a former chemist, I absolutely loved the hundreds of bottles of chemicals that pharmacists used to use to mix their medicines. I also loved the old, marble soda fountain, and couldn't recall ever seeing an earlier version. But the real highlight of this building is what Lori refers to as "the vortex." I didn't quite understand what she meant, until I found myself a little light-headed, and suddenly and inexplicably leaning to my right. I took two steps away from that spot and the feeling ceased. Is there some strong, natural electromagnetic force in the ground under this building, or is this some strong, spiritual force that messes with your mind and equilibrium?

We next went into the original, 18th century log cabin, which Roscoe Smith had dismantled and transported from where it had been built in Dean Mine, five miles west of Fort Montgomery, New York. Despite the somewhat cramped confines of the interior, the atmosphere was quite nice, and I considered this to be a happy place for spirits. Had the former inhabitants lead good, full lives, and remained with the building to continue to experience a time when they were happy…and alive?

The interior of the log cabin.

No, this is not haunted goat, just a happy inhabitant of Museum Village.

Our last stop had nothing to do with any ghosts, but had everything to do with me being a science geek. Many people, including myself, are surprised to find out that Museum Village holds one of only three of the most complete mastodon skeletons known in the world. Harry, as he is affectionately known (because he was discovered in Harriman, New York, in 1952), stands majestically in a large building which also houses a re-creation of a giant sloth skeleton, as well as a mineral collection, including fluorescent minerals (another thing the science geek in me loves!). Lori said that she tells schoolchildren to imagine Harry roaming this very land thousands of years ago, which he and his mastodon friends must have done, as his skeleton was discovered just two miles away.

All in all, I was quite delighted with my visit to Museum Village, and had an entirely new appreciation for the place since I last visited as a kid many years ago. Of course, what would put the icing on the cake would be to return with Mike Worden and Barbara Bleitzhofer for a complete investigation. Fortunately, that opportunity presented itself just a short time later.

Harry used to walk around Harriman and Monroe, NY.

I arranged for us to return on July 6 for a second investigation with Barbara and Mike. We would also have some special guest investigators—Mike's twin boys, Ryan and Michael, who would be conducting their first official ghost hunt! In the true spirit of introducing rookie paranormal investigators to the realm of the 'other' world, I immediately informed Ryan and Michael that we would be shamelessly using them as "ghost bait," especially in the schoolhouse!

Our team: (l-r) Ryan, Michael, and me, Barbara, and Mike.

We all arrived in the evening, and Barbara had obviously already hit the ground running as she told me that as soon as she got to the parking lot, a tall, thin figure of a man came out of one of the buildings and walked right up to her car! He was dressed "like an undertaker" and she felt that his nickname had been "Digger." Barb also had taken some notes, as the night before she had been contacted by a man with a name starting with "Emer," and as we were to find out later, she was dead on, as always.

Before beginning on the night's activities, however, I do want to point out something that happened, which literally started out our night with a bang. Mike and the boys had picked me up at my house, and on the way to Museum Village, we stopped behind a car at an intersection. For some unknown reason, that car pulled halfway out into the road, where traffic was traveling at a very high rate of speed. The driver then stopped in the middle of the lane of traffic, and an approaching car slammed on its brakes.

The driver of that vehicle did her best to avoid an accident, but unfortunately there was a collision. Had that second driver not so skillfully maneuvered her car, she would have hit our vehicle head on, as well. It was a close call for us, but the important thing is that both drivers were unhurt, and it certainly got our adrenaline pumping before we even arrived at Museum Village.

Lori was in the office to greet us, along with fellow staff member Holly Moylan, and we were soon geared up and ready to go. As the grounds are so extensive, and there are so many buildings, I decided to present our findings by location. Some of the buildings we went in twice, both before and after dark, so this is not a strictly chronological report of the night's events.

Mike took this photo of our group around sunset as we went to the many buildings at Museum Village.

Vernon Drugstore: When Lori unlocked the front door, Barb started to enter, but paused as she said she already felt woozy from the energies inside. I asked if she was all right and whether she wanted me to go in first, but she took a moment and proceeded—and went right to the spot near the stove that has the most intense activity; where I had an experience on my first visit, and where Lori believes there is a portal or vortex.

"There's a woman, a woman…whoa!" Barb exclaimed, swaying back and forth. "She passed away from some respiratory problems. She was very grumpy, and I'm just going to say it like it is—don't piss her off! She came here by wagon and I feel like she's from the frontier times, early 1800s."

While this grumpy woman is the overwhelming presence here, Barb also felt that there was a man in a checkered shirt, who likes to be called Chuck, who sits by the stove. Lori pointed out that the man who owned this Drugstore in Florida, New York, was Charles Vernon—perhaps nicknamed Chuck?

We all felt some strong energy in that building after dark, when we returned to do some filming in infrared. I half-jokingly asked if one of the boys would like to sit on the floor near the stove, on possibly *the most* intense single hot spot location on the property, and was both surprised and delighted that Michael didn't hesitate to go right over to the stove and sit down, while Ryan moved forward with his infrared camcorder to film his brother.

"Good for you!" I said, certain that most adults I knew would not have the courage to be doing what these two boys were at that moment, in the dark of a haunted drugstore.

It was actually their father, though, Mike, who would have the first brush with the paranormal—literally! I was sitting against the front of one of the counters, and he was sitting behind the counter, when I heard him jump. At that same instant, Barbara said that she saw a short, white figure rush by Mike, and he said whatever it was had brushed against his leg as it passed.

"Why didn't you warn me?" Mike asked Barbara, laughing at the shock and surprise of the sudden and unpleasant contact. "Thanks, Barb!"

"I didn't have time!" Barb replied. "It was moving too fast."

I asked if anyone was there who used to work in the drugstore, and we all heard a tapping sound behind Michael. Just to make sure it wasn't the old, wood floor creaking, he moved back and forth several times, but no similar sound was generated. He was then even brave enough to ask for someone to make a noise, or even tap him on the shoulder! A moment later, he tapped on the floor and asked for a response, and we all heard another tap behind him! It certainly appeared as though something had directly responded.

Michael sits in the "vortex" while Ryan films him in infrared.
Photo courtesy of Barbara Bleitzhofer.

We were going to continue this line of questioning, when Barb suddenly shouted, "Oh, Lord!" and lurched backward. We all jumped to our feet and moved toward the door, as we had no idea what had so startled her. Let me assure you, when your psychic is alarmed by something, you all instinctively retreat and get ready to make a hasty exit if necessary.

Barb explained that a dark, shadowy, male figure rose up behind her, and then moved onto the ceiling. The figure then appeared to expand and get larger, spreading out across the ceiling and toward the back of the drugstore. The atmosphere in the store suddenly shifted to one of nasty negativity, and we felt as though we were no longer welcome in there.

We went outside to talk to Lori and Holly, who were sitting on a nearby bench, and Barb explained what she had seen. Both women acknowledged that they had seen a similar black, shadowy figure in the livery stable one night. Lori saw it as a human-sized figure, but Holly saw it move and grow to the size of the back wall of the stable! This was the same thing that Barbara had just experienced; the dark figure of a man which had the ability to spread across an entire ceiling or wall.

As we discussed this mysterious shadow figure, we heard a loud noise from *inside* the drugstore. We were about 10 yards away, so I decided to go up to the front door to hear or see what I could. However, as I reached the door, I got the distinct and overwhelming feeling that whatever was inside did not want me there. It didn't need to tell me twice, and so we were done with the drugstore, at least for this investigation.

I *love* this old soda fountain in the drugstore!

Log Cabin: I had felt that this cabin was a happy place, or at least very comfortable and nonthreatening. Barb felt that there was a little girl, around five or six years old, who had been one of the original residents when it was built in the 1700s.

She also kept hearing a woman repeatedly telling a man to "mind your Ps and Qs." It is a phrase which has a variety of possible origins, but Barb felt that in this case it meant pints and quarts, as in drinking ale. I suggested that the man of the house drank too much, and as I spoke those words, my K2 meter lit up! I had apparently touched on a very sensitive subject.

Natural History Building: This is where Harry the mastodon now resides, but Barbara didn't get any particular sensations from the old bones. The two things of interest in this building were the old grinding stones. When she placed her hands on them, Barb said she could just hear women sitting around the stones, noisily chattering.

Firehouse: This was a building I hadn't entered on my first visit, so I was quite pleased to see the impressive collection of old firefighting equipment. I was also very thankful that we live in an age of such modern firetrucks, as I would not want to have my life and property rest upon an old horse-drawn pumper wagon!

"Frank. Frank is here," Barbara said with certainty, as we entered the building.

The 1840 Washington Pumper.

Lori asked if he was connected to anything in particular, and after thinking for a few moments, Barbara pointed to the 1840 Washington Pumper. As she did this, the EMF meters that Ryan and I were holding lit up.

However, when Lori asked if Frank liked the postcards they had of that pumper, both of our EMF meters went dark. I said that I thought it was odd that Frank apparently didn't like the postcards of the piece of equipment with which he had such an attachment, but Lori quickly cleared that up issue.

"I agree with Frank, they're terrible," she explained, alluding to the poor quality of the postcards. "I don't blame him if he doesn't like them."

Holly asked if she should just give them away to children, and our EMF meters lit up again! Frank not only had decidedly strong opinions, but also the ability to express them! As we have seen on other cases—such as the Montgomery Firehouse story in this book—being a firefighter is a great source of pride, and it's a job many of them take beyond the grave with them, at least in spirit!

Mike took this photo of Ryan (r.) and I with our K2 meters which appeared to be responding to "Frank" the fireman.

Monroe Journal Job Printing: This building holds some very impressive printing presses and equipment. Lori demonstrated how one of the presses works, and showed us samples of the printed material it still generates after over 100 years of operation. (Wouldn't it be nice if things today were made to last a century?)

Barb felt that a man who used to run that particular press had died from the toxic effects of the inks and chemicals they used in the past. I later did some research on safety hazards in the printing industry, and even today, many of the solvents used pose serious health issues, so it is entirely possible that in the past, long-term exposure could have been dangerous.

The press to which the spirit is attached.

It was at this point that we began discussing the man that came to Barbara the night before, with the name that started with "Emer." He was a very strong presence just about everywhere we went that evening. Lori and Holly said that a man named Emerick had worked there for many years, and that Museum Village was "his home away from home" before he passed away. By the end of the night, we were convinced that it is still his home!

Merritt General Store: First of all, Mike complained that his camera was taking blurry pictures in several locations, and Barbara and I both agreed were we having the same problems, and that this was very unusual for the cameras we were using. Inside the general store, all three of us had problems again, with the majority of our photos being out of focus. It didn't make sense, so we just had to take a lot of extra pictures to make sure we at least got a few good ones.

We also felt very uncomfortable, with an unpleasant feeling of pressure and pain in our heads. Near one of the counters, Barb felt a particularly strong pain. It is not a word she uses very often, but she described the feeling at this spot as being "evil." There was something connected to one of the items in that area that was generating this nasty energy. The rest of the building felt fine, but not in that one spot on that night.

Barb is distressed in the spot of the negative energy.

Livery Stable: There was a powerful energy again in the livery stable. Mike tried setting up his Trifield EMF meter on one of the hearses, but he could not adjust it to stop its alarm from going off. And the alarm was sounding in a most unusual manner that none of us had ever heard before; a kind of staccato chattering. Barbara felt that the man she first encountered upon arriving, Digger, stands by this particular hearse.

Whether or not it was Digger, something was certainly there, affecting the EMF meter.

Barb placed her hand on one of the other hearses and immediately gasped. I asked what was wrong, and she said she saw a "corpse with no eyes" inside the hearse! He was wearing some type of uniform, and somehow his "eyes had been gouged out." That image would have sent most people running, but Barb kind of smiled and simply remarked what a cool image it was.

Barbara by the hearse with the eyeless corpse.

A few moments later, there was a loud sound *inside* the building that we all described as a deep thud. It was loud enough to be captured by my audio recorder, although we couldn't find the source of the sound, and it did not occur again. And let me impress upon you that when you are standing in the dark near old hearses that carried countless bodies to their graves, such a sound is quite memorable!

Schoolhouse: On my first visit, Lori had told me about Claire, the little girl with the long, blond pigtails that both she and a guard had seen as clear as day. When we all entered the schoolhouse that evening, Barbara immediately said there was a little girl named Annie, and that her most distinguishing feature was her "long, blond pigtails." No one is quite sure where the name Claire originated, but in the future I think they'll need to refer to her as Annie.

Our EMF meters lit up several times when we mentioned Claire/Annie, and it really did feel as if we were not alone. Barbara felt that there were as many as five children's spirits in and around the schoolhouse, and they appeared to like Michael in particular, who at one point said that he felt that a little girl had sat next to him.

The schoolhouse was definitely a place worth more of our time, but as something had apparently died nearby, the smell of 'decomp' on that warm, humid evening was too much to take for very long. We were compelled to say good night to Annie and her friends, and hoped that someday we would be back on a less fragrant occasion.

Barbara's photo of Mike, Michael, and me in the schoolhouse.

Wagon Repair: Another hearse with curved glass windows is housed in the wagon repair building. This was not a building we were allowed to walk through. However, just standing near the hearse gave us the creeps.

"This one has a lot of negativity are around it," Barbara said, holding onto her aching head.

She said that someone who had been carried in this hearse had been killed by being shot in the chest, and as she said that, our EMF meters lit up again. Of the four hearses on the property, this one was definitely the most disturbing.

Gift Shop: After the intolerable odor by the schoolhouse, the pleasant aroma of wood was a welcome change inside of the Gift Shop. This is where Holly works, and Barbara informed her that she was never alone in this building. Holly was naturally curious as to who was there with her, and Barbara went on to describe the character and mannerisms of an older woman. Both Holly and Lori agreed that Barbara had just described "to a

T" a woman who had worked there for more than 25 years, well into her late nineties, and had just recently passed about a year ago.

The woman had worked in this particular building when it was the weaver's shop, and one of her looms was still there. Barbara always works best when she is able to touch an object, so she placed her hands on the loom and started laughing.

"She keeps saying, 'Don't touch me!' over and over," Barbara announced, which caused Lori and Holly to gasp.

"That's what she always said!" Lori exclaimed in surprise. "Even when she was old and kind of wobbly on her feet, she wouldn't let anybody help her because she didn't want to be touched!"

Once again, we had some EMF activity while speaking about this very talented, but somewhat eccentric, weaver, who obviously still occupied the building.

Other than that ominous, black, shadowy figure, the picture that had developed over the course of my two visits was of people who loved their time here and very much felt part of the place—so much so that even after death, this is where they choose to spend their time.

And speaking of loving this place, I would be remiss if I didn't again mention the founder himself, Roscoe Smith. He has been seen and felt throughout the property, and when Barbara looked at his photo in the main office at the end of our investigation, she was certain he was one of the spirits she saw walking around and sitting on the benches. And as Barbara was talking about Roscoe, we heard a strange sound, almost as if someone was giggling or laughing, so maybe he was amused by our presence and all the attention. With Roscoe, as with many of the spirits at Museum Village, perhaps the old saying of "You can't take it with you" should be amended to "You can't take it with you, but you can come back for it!"

I have saved the most remarkable experience of the evening, at least for me, for last. It did not take place in any of the buildings, but as we were walking through the darkness toward the schoolhouse to pick up the camcorder Mike had left running inside. As we were passing two old steam engine tractors, there was a loud, metallic, scraping sound that made us all stop in our tracks and turn at once like a school of fish. It was a startling, jarring sound, which had the same unnerving effect on us as fingernails on a blackboard.

One of the old steam engines where we heard the scraping sound.

I turned to say something to Barbara and saw a man walking behind her in a black suit with a white shirt and no tie. He was a thin, gangly figure, and his clothes were decidedly ill-fitting, but he was so real and solid that I assumed I was looking at a real person. Until he vanished! I was so surprised that I ended up turning completely around, but he was nowhere to be seen. He was walking quickly across the grass one second, and the next second he disappeared into thin air.

Before I could say what I had just witnessed, Barbara pointed right at me and said, "You saw him, too, didn't you? It was a tall man in a suit, who was sitting on this bench, and then he got up and hurried off in that direction and just disappeared."

I didn't see the man when he was sitting on the bench, but I told her that I certainly did see him walking passed her and then vanishing. Lori and Holly were back in the main office when this occurred, but when we got back I explained what I had seen and described the figure as "looking like Ichabod Crane."

At the same time, they both said they knew exactly who it was; a man who had worked there for many years and had only died just a month or two earlier. They said he very much looked like Ichabod Crane, and his clothes never quite seemed to fit properly. So once again, here was an example of someone who poured his heart and soul into this living history museum, and wouldn't even let death prevent him from remaining here.

This was a fitting end to a remarkable evening, and I summed up all of the activity here by saying, "You don't see full-bodied apparitions every day of the week." Although, if I worked at Museum Village, perhaps I would!

I strongly urge you to visit Museum Village with your entire family, even if you have no interest in the paranormal. The time, effort, and devotion of so many people went into the creation of this remarkable museum, and you truly feel like you are stepping back in time. And if you *do* have an interest in the paranormal, what are you doing sitting there reading this book, when you should be getting in the car and heading for an incredible experience that you will never forget?

Finally, for those of you who truly look upon fear as entertainment, mark your calendars this Halloween season for their Screampark experience. But just remember, all the ghosts you see there might not be people in costumes.

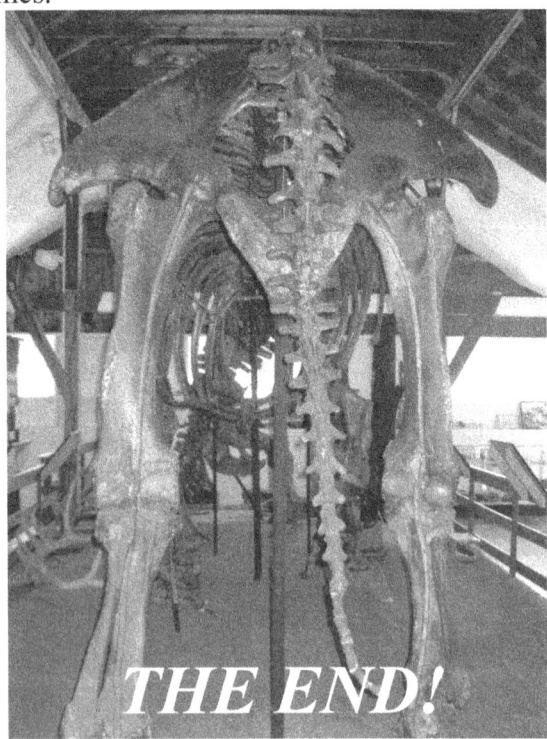

Copy this page to use for your own ghost hunt. If you know of a haunted site you think should be considered for an upcoming book, please contact me at:
P.O. Box 192, Blooming Grove, NY, 10914
www.ghostinvestigator.com

Field Report

Date: **Location:**

Time In: **Weather:**

Names of People Interviewed:

Equipment: Camera ☐ **Video** ☐ **Audio Recorder** ☐ **Thermometer**   **Other:**

Experiences: Sounds ☐   Odors ☐   Cold Spots ☐   Visuals ☐   Touch/Sensations ☐   Movement ☐

Details (Attach extra sheet if necessary):

Time Out: **Total Time on Site:**

Conclusions:

Prepared and Signed by:

Witness(es):

Other books by Linda Zimmermann

Available in print and as e-books on Amazon and B&N
For more info and to order autographed copies:
www.gotozim.com

Dead Center
A Ghost Hunter Novel

When one of the country's largest shopping centers is built in Virginia, rumors abound that the place is haunted by ghosts of Civil War soldiers. Ghost hunter Sarah Brooks must uncover the truth, and come face to face with the restless spirits that walk through the *Dead Center*:

Okay, Sarah Brooks. This is what you do, she said to herself. *This is who you are.*

Closing her eyes, Sarah spun around and counted to three. When she opened her eyes, she had to clamp her hand over her mouth to stifle a scream. There was a pale, misty shape of a man drawing closer. It was like an image being projected into a fog, and it rippled, wavered, then slowly began to take on a more defined shape. The wounded man behind her screamed as if Death himself was coming to take him…

Ghost Investigator Series

Ghost Investigator Volume 1:
Hauntings of the Hudson Valley

Ghost Investigator Volume 2:
From Gettysburg to Lizzie Borden

Ghost Investigator Volume 3

Ghost Investigator Volume 4:
Ghosts of New York and New Jersey

Ghost Investigator Volume 5:
From Beyond the Grave

Ghost Investigator Volume 6:
Dark Shadows

Ghost Investigator Volume 7:
Psychic Impressions

Ghost Investigator Volume 8:
Back Into the Light

Ghost Investigator Volume 9:
Back from the Dead

Ghost Investigator Volume 10

Ghost Investigator Volume 11

Ghost Investigator Volume 12

Ghost Investigator 10th Anniversary Special Edition:
Favorite Haunts

Ghosts of Rockland County:
Collected Stories Edition

Hudson Valley Haunts: Historic Driving Tours

New York's Hudson River Valley is a place of captivating beauty and fascinating history. It is also one of the most haunted regions in the country. From ancient Indian spirits at Spook Rock, to soldiers still walking the battlefield of Fort Montgomery, to the many haunted houses that line the streets of the old Dutch settlements in New Paltz and Hurley, this book has something extra to offer tourists—ghosts that still make their presence known to those who dare to visit.

What greater adventure can there be then to go to such a site, explore the rich history of its people and the events, and then see if you can discover any deeper secrets from the other world, where a passing shadow or faint whisper may signal that you have just had an encounter in the haunted Hudson Valley.

America's Historic Haunts

From remote villages in Alaska, to ancient Native American settlements in the southwest, to an old Spanish town in Florida, and bustling metropolitan areas in the northeast, follow the fascinating trail of historic haunts across the country. Test your ghost hunting skills in an old prison or fort, dine in restaurants where paranormal activity is on the menu, and sleep in some of America's most haunted inns. Whether you're a frequent flier or an armchair adventurer, this book will take you on a journey of discovery into the people, places, and events that led to the spirits that still walk among us in some of this country's greatest travel destinations.

Ghost Investigator
The Comic Book
Issue #1
Available at: www.comicfleamarket.com
Issue #2 available at:
www.outpouringcomics.com

In the Night Sky and *Hudson Valley UFOs*

Eyewitness accounts of classic flying saucers, giant, silent triangles, and possible abductions in one of the most active UFO areas of the country.

The film *In the Night Sky: I Recall a UFO* based on the book was the winner of the People's Choice Award at the EBE Film Festival at the 2013 International UFO Congress.

HVZA and HVZA 2:
Hudson Valley Zombie Apocalypse

Amazon.com Reviews:

"GREAT book. Buy it; you won't regret it. Well... except maybe for at 3 AM when you're either A) still up reading because can't put this page-turner down or B) waking up out of a zombie nightmare because the characters and situations in the book can seem so REAL. But buy it anyway."

"You relate, you get sucked in, seriously it's been a while since I enjoyed a book so much."

"The author has an uncanny ability to pull you into the story and make you feel like you are there."

"Zimmermann really hits home with her depiction of life during the collapse of civilization, and the heart wrenching losses, choices and sacrifices that people must make in order to survive. Zimmermann is a master manipulator of emotions: the love, fear, sadness, pain, and suffering of the various characters are surprisingly real. Set in the Hudson Valley, the authentic locations and settings lend an additional layer of realism that so many other works of fiction neglect. These just are not zombies that are attacking people - these are zombies that are attacking your neighbors and family and friends."

HVZA:
Hudson Valley Zombie Apocalypse

THE GRAPHIC NOVEL

"A truly imaginative Zombie Anthology. Full of stories for every appetite."
-- Paul J. Salamoff, Writer/Producer (Discord, Logan's Run: Last Day)

"Not since peanut butter and chocolate has there been as perfect a combination as zombies and comics! What's better than one zombie story? How about a whole brain-eating collection of zombie stories?!"
--Jim Salicrup, Editor-in-Chief, Papercutz and former Marvel Comics editor on "The Avengers," "The Amazing Spider-Man," "The Uncanny X-Men" and "The Fantastic Four."

Bad Science:
A Brief History of Bizarre Misconceptions, Totally Wrong Conclusions, and Incredibly Stupid Theories

Winner of the 2011 Silver Medal for Humor
in the international Independent Publisher Awards

Amazon.com Review:

"*Bad Science* is simultaneously informative and ever-so-entertaining. Riveting! Enthralling! Hilarious! I highly recommend this book if you like a jaw dropping read that is a LAUGH OUT LOUD."

WWW.GOTOZIM.COM

www.ingramcontent.com/pod-product-compliance
Lightning Source LLC
Chambersburg PA
CBHW032139040426
42449CB00005B/321